Enjoy The Fear

Absolute Deliverance from Fear

Gajendra Singh Rathore

ISBN: 978-93-344-5235-8

This book is a work of personal reflection. While inspired by genuine experiences, insights, and spiritual understanding, it is not intended to replace professional psychological, medical, or spiritual advice. Readers are encouraged to interpret the ideas in the context of their own life and understanding.

This book integrates insights from both ancient philosophical traditions and modern scientific research. All scientific concepts mentioned, such as brain regions, neural responses, and physiological processes, are drawn from publicly available knowledge in the fields of neuroscience and psychology.

The interpretations, explanations, and metaphors presented herein are original reflections of the author, intended to promote awareness, understanding, and personal growth.

This work is not a substitute for professional medical or psychological advice. Readers experiencing persistent stress, anxiety, or mental health concerns are encouraged to seek qualified professional guidance.

DEDICATION

This book is dedicated to every soul who wakes each morning with a storm in the mind, to those who silently carry the weight of unseen fears, unspoken worries, and unanswered questions, yet still choose to move forward each day.

It is for those who have felt the tremor of anxiety in their chest, the pressure of decisions left untaken, and the quiet loneliness that sometimes follows doubt and overthinking. To you who continue to rise, to work, to hope, even when the mind whispers uncertainty, this book belongs to you.

It is also a bow of gratitude to **GuruDev Sri Sri Ravi Shankar**, whose boundless wisdom revealed that peace does not come from escaping the noise of life, but from awakening within it. Through his guidance, I learned that fear is not an enemy to defeat, but a doorway to awareness, a passage into the heart of silence.

To my wife, whose listening heart and simple words gave life to this journey. That evening, when our conversation turned to fear, what it means, where it hides, and how it can dissolve, something profound awakened within me. Her calm acceptance and quiet faith reflected the truth that love itself can dissolve the deepest anxiety.

And finally, to every reader who seeks to understand rather than escape their inner storms, may these pages remind you that courage is not the absence of fear. It is the grace to walk through it with open eyes, a steady breath, and faith in the divine intelligence within.

May you discover, as I did,
that fear was never here to imprison you
it was here to awaken you.

CONTENTS

ACKNOWLEDGMENTS

The journey that led to this book began long ago. From 1998 to 2025, I lived under the silent weight of tension, fear, and self-created pressure, always trying to stay ahead, to achieve more, to secure what I already had. For years, I mistook worry for responsibility and fear for motivation, without realizing how deeply it was draining my peace and joy.

Everything changed when **Gurudev Sri Sri Ravi Shankar** came into my life. Through his wisdom and the daily practice of *Dhyan*, Yoga, and meditation, my mind began to quiet, and a new kind of knowledge started arising from within, effortlessly, naturally, and often beyond logic. Whenever such insights came, I would share them with my wife. She would listen with calm curiosity, often smiling in surprise, saying, "How are you discovering all this? Is this truly from meditation?"

Those conversations became the seed of this book. Her quiet encouragement and Gurudev's grace turned years of struggle into understanding.

To Gurudev, for showing me that fear itself can become a doorway to freedom, and to my wife, for her steady faith and presence, my deepest gratitude.

PREFACE

Fear has always been a companion of human existence. It hides behind ambition, lurks beneath uncertainty, and often stands between who we are and who we wish to become. For centuries, people have been taught to overcome it, suppress it, or escape from it. Yet few have ever been shown how to understand it.

This book was written to change that conversation. In modern life, fear no longer wears dramatic forms. It is subtle, appearing as anxiety before a meeting, hesitation before making a decision, or sleepless restlessness that has no name. We live in a time where technology has simplified everything except the human mind. Knowledge is expanding, but peace is shrinking. People have mastered tools that reach across the world, yet many struggle to master the quiet space within themselves.

Enjoy the Fear was born from observing this paradox. It is not a book about positive thinking or forced optimism. It is a guide to understanding how fear, stress, and anxiety function within the architecture of the mind, and how they can become sources of growth instead of suffering. The idea is simple but transformative- fear exists not to stop us but to refine us. It is a signal from the deeper intelligence of life, asking us to awaken, to pay attention, and to participate consciously in our evolution.

This book is for those who are tired of temporary relief. It is for anyone who has experienced the weight of mental overthinking, the paralysis of indecision, or the silent panic of uncertainty. It offers a perspective that neither denies nor glorifies fear but treats it as a sacred teacher. Through understanding, surrender, and awareness, one can transform fear into clarity, anxiety into energy, and stress into wisdom.

The chapters that follow will move gradually, from the anatomy of thoughts and emotions to the art of surrender and the rediscovery of divine connection. The purpose is not merely to inspire, but to help you see yourself clearly, to realize that fear has never been your enemy. It has always been your messenger, guiding you toward balance, presence, and freedom.

If there is one truth that unites every page of this book, it is that peace does not come from control; it comes from understanding. Once you learn to enjoy the presence of fear, to observe it without panic, you step into a dimension of inner strength that remains untouched by external chaos.

This book does not promise a life without fear. It offers something greater- a life where fear loses its power to rule you.

INTRODUCTION

Meaning of Fear-

Every human being carries two invisible companions through life, hope and fear. Hope pushes us forward; fear holds us back. Yet, somewhere between these two, we spend most of our lives trying to survive instead of truly living. For years, I too lived this way, chasing deadlines, achievements, and recognition, believing that if I could control every uncertainty, I would finally be at peace. But peace never came. The more I tried to control life, the more restless it became. That restlessness, which we often call anxiety or stress, is not created by life itself; it is created by our resistance to how life unfolds.

The idea behind Enjoy the Fear is simple- fear is not an obstacle, it is a teacher. It reveals what we truly value and where we are not yet free. Most people spend their lives running away from it, hiding behind distractions, possessions, or work. But fear does not disappear when ignored; it simply changes its form. It shows up as irritation, overthinking, comparison, or even physical pain. This book was not written to give you quick relief. It was written to help you understand the inner mechanics of fear, where it comes from, why it exists, and how to transform it. Because the truth is, fear is not a mistake in creation. It is part of divine design. Without it, there would be no awareness, no caution, no learning, no growth.

Over time, through meditation and the grace of my Guru, I realized that fear dissolves not by fighting it, but by observing it. When you witness fear with a calm and steady mind, something miraculous happens, the same energy that once terrified you begins to awaken intelligence within you. You start seeing fear not as an enemy, but as a form of guidance. In the chapters ahead, we will explore this journey from resistance to awareness. You will learn how thoughts create the illusion of fear, how surrender connects you to a higher intelligence, and how understanding this connection changes the way you experience life.

This is not a religious book, but it is deeply spiritual. It speaks to every human being who has ever worried about the future, doubted their own strength, or lost themselves in the noise of the world. It invites you to experience life as it is, without the constant need to protect, compare, or prove. If you read this book slowly, reflect on its questions, and practice even a few of its insights, you will notice something subtle but powerful, your mind will begin to relax. You will stop trying to eliminate fear and instead start listening to what it wants to teach you. That is when true transformation begins.

So as you turn these pages, I invite you not to fight your fear, but to befriend it. Let it show you who you are beneath the noise of thoughts and expectations. The day you learn to enjoy fear, you will realize it was never here to harm you, it was here to make you whole.

PART- I

THE NATURE OF FEAR

1 THE BIRTH OF FEAR

Before thought began, before words existed, life was already aware of itself. Every living form, from the smallest organism to the first beating heart, carried within it a quiet knowing: that life could end. From that awareness, a movement arose, gentle yet powerful, the movement toward protection. That was the beginning of fear.

In its earliest expression, fear was simple and honest. When a spark of heat touched the skin, the body pulled away. When a sound broke the stillness, the eyes opened wide. Fear was not something imagined; it was the body's way of recognizing life and preserving it.

When a newborn cries for the first time, it is not weakness. It is the beginning of connection, the body's call for warmth, breath, and safety. That sound marks the entry of awareness into a fragile world. Fear is already there, but not as suffering; rather as a sign that life values itself enough to hold on.

As time passed and the human mind began to remember, compare, and imagine, fear changed its form. What once kept our ancestors alert to the rustle in the dark now whispers about tomorrow, about what might go wrong, about what could be lost. The same ancient signal of care began to echo in the chambers of imagination, where no real danger existed.

In this way, fear slowly left the body and found a home in thought. It began to live between memory and expectation, no longer a momentary reaction to life, but a constant commentary about it. And yet, beneath all this complexity, its original purpose remains the same: to keep life aware of itself.

When we call fear "bad," we overlook its intelligence. It speaks in the only language it knows, caution, attention, care. It reminds us that what we love is fragile, that time moves, that existence is fleeting. In that sense, fear and love are never far apart. What we fear losing is often what we love most.

To understand fear, we must see it not as a flaw in our nature, but as a companion that has travelled with us since the beginning. It is part of the same rhythm that drives the heartbeat and draws the breath. When we stop resisting it, it becomes quiet, almost tender, an ally instead of an adversary.

This is where our journey begins: not with the attempt to silence fear, but with the willingness to understand it. Only by seeing where it came from, and how it continues to serve life, can we begin to transform it from tension into awareness, from defense into wisdom.

Evolutionary Roots of Fear-

Fear did not arrive late to human life; it arrived first. Long before language, culture, or even complex social structures, organisms survived because they could detect and respond to threat. In this sense, fear is not a moral failing or a psychological glitch. It is a form of biological intelligence, an exquisitely tuned early-warning system that has been selected and refined across millions of years. The species that sensed danger a fraction of a second earlier were the species that lived to reproduce. That advantage accumulated, generation after generation, until it became woven into our nervous system as reliably as heartbeat and breath.

At its simplest level, fear is detection plus preparation. Organisms detect deviation from safety, sudden movement, unfamiliar shapes, looming shadows, abrupt sounds, changes in temperature or proximity, and then prepare the body to respond. Even single reflexes reveal this logic. The startle response in infants (the Moro reflex), the blink to an unexpected puff of air, the flinch from rapid approach- these are not learned behaviors. They are preinstalled programs that favor survival. In later development, the same architecture becomes more sophisticated; it still detects the unexpected, but it also predicts it.

Humans are predictive beings. The brain is constantly comparing incoming signals with its internal model of the world, asking a single question- "Is everything as expected?" Fear emerges when the answer is "No," or when the cost of being wrong is high. That is why fear is closely tied to uncertainty. A rustle in tall grass is ambiguous; it could be the wind or a predator. The intelligent move, from an evolutionary standpoint, is to assume the worst and act quickly. The price of a false alarm is small; the price of ignoring a real threat is catastrophic. This asymmetry, small cost for caution, huge cost for negligence, shaped our threat systems into what they are today- conservative, fast, and sometimes overprotective.

The body's preparation routines are equally intelligent. When the system flags a threat, it reallocates resources instantly. The sympathetic nervous system elevates heart rate and blood pressure to deliver oxygen and glucose to the large muscles; pupils dilate to take in more light; non-essential processes (digestion, complex digestion-related secretions, reproductive functions) downshift to conserve energy; blood coagulation factors increase in case of injury; attention narrows to relevant cues while background noise fades. None of this is a "panic mistake." It is a purpose-built configuration that prioritizes speed, strength, and focus over reflection, because in a genuine emergency, analysis is slower than action.

Crucially, fear is not only about external predators or physical harm. Evolution also selected for sensitivity to social and environmental dangers. For social species like ours, exclusion, status loss, and rejection historically carried real survival costs- fewer allies, less protection, reduced access to resources and mates. The brain therefore uses the same circuitry to flag social risks that it uses for physical threats. That is why a harsh email or a public criticism can create bodily sensations similar to standing on the edge of a cliff- a tightening of the chest, a surge of heat, a cascade of vigilance. The system is agnostic to the source; what matters is possible loss.

This helps explain why fear and learning are entwined. The nervous system marks threat-associated situations with priority tags so they are remembered better and avoided in the future. A child touches a hot surface once and acquires a durable caution. The chemistry of fear, adrenaline, noradrenaline, cortisol, does not only mobilize muscles; it strengthens certain forms of memory, particularly those that link context with consequence. In ancestral environments, that was wisdom- remember the bend in the river where crocodiles wait; store the pattern of clouds that precedes a violent storm; recognize the facial expression that has predicted aggression before. Fear, used properly, is the fast teacher.

Because of this teaching function, fear is not inherently "negative." It is directional. It pushes us away from peril and toward safety. It sharpens the senses, improves reaction time, and limits distraction. In moderation, that same arousal improves performance in complex tasks, the well-known inverted-U relationship between arousal and effectiveness.

Too little alertness and we are sluggish; too much and we are scattered; in the middle band, we are precise. Athletes, surgeons, pilots, and performers learn to ride that band, to translate the body's fear energy into concentration. What they call being "in the zone" is often a refined conversation with the very machinery that evolution built for survival.

The anatomy behind this intelligence is straightforward in concept, even if complex in detail. Sensory data streams through thalamic relays; rapid, coarse threat signals can take a fast track to the amygdala, which triggers autonomic responses before the slower cortical systems have fully interpreted the scene. This two-path design, quick and rough, then slower and detailed, ensures we can move first and explain later. Meanwhile, the hippocampus encodes context ("where was I when this happened?"), and the prefrontal cortex evaluates options, inhibiting or permitting actions based on goals, rules, and longer-term consequences. When conditions are truly dangerous, subcortical urgency appropriately outweighs cortical debate. When conditions are safe, prefrontal guidance dampens unnecessary alarms. In a healthy system, this balance is dynamic.

Modern environments complicate the picture. Our bodies still deploy ancient responses, but the threats we encounter are less about sudden predators and more about chronic ambiguity, financial uncertainty, organizational politics, social comparison, information overload. The same biological intelligence works here too- it flags uncertainty, narrows attention, and prepares the body. But because these threats are ongoing and abstract, the preparation has no clear endpoint. Muscles brace for a sprint that never starts; the mind searches endlessly for a resolution it cannot find. What was once a short burst of mobilization becomes a long simmer of vigilance. We experience that simmer as "stress," "anxiety," or "constant pressure," but it is still the same ancient intelligence trying to be useful in a world it did not evolve to predict.

Understanding fear as biological intelligence helps dissolve shame. Many people interpret their fearful reactions as personal weakness- "Why am I like this?" The more accurate question is, "What is my system trying to accomplish?" It is trying to keep you alive, socially connected, and out of irreversible harm. It is cautious by design. It errs on the side of over-alerting because the cost of missing a real threat has been, across evolutionary time, too great.

Recognizing this changes our relationship to the sensations of fear. Rather than resisting or resenting them, we can treat them as information, sometimes miscalibrated, often helpful, and always worthy of respectful attention.

Respect does not mean obedience. Biological intelligence can be guided. Just as we train reflexes in sport or performance, we can train how the system interprets signals and how quickly it returns to baseline after mobilization. Habits that improve sleep, regulate breath, and clarify attention all feed back into the threat circuitry. Slow, controlled exhalations stimulate parasympathetic tone and shorten recovery time after arousal. Repeated exposures to manageable challenges recalibrate what the amygdala treats as "dangerous." Clear, values-based decisions reduce the number of unresolved uncertainties that keep the system in a half-alarmed state. In other words, the same evolutionary apparatus that once kept us from predators can be educated to serve modern flourishing.

It is also important to see that fear collaborates with other forms of intelligence. Curiosity, for instance, is fear's sibling. Both are heightened responses to the unexpected, one leans toward approach, the other toward avoidance. In balanced systems, they alternate productively- fear pauses us to assess, curiosity moves us to explore; fear protects the boundary, curiosity expands it. Creativity often arises at that border. Too little fear and we behave recklessly; too much and we never attempt what could change our lives. The art of living, then, is not eliminating fear, but coordinating it, allowing its signal to inform without dictating, to prepare without imprisoning.

Seen in this light, the biological story of fear is not a story of pathology; it is a story of adaptation. Our ancestors handed us a nervous system that cares deeply about continuity, safety, and belonging. It scans for the unknown, it rehearses contingencies, it stores lessons with priority tags. When it overshoots, when it treats an email like a tiger or a presentation like a cliff, it is misapplied intelligence, not malice. The correction begins with understanding- "My system is doing its job; now I will help it do the right job."

This reframe matters for everything that follows in this book. If we start by calling fear "bad," we fight our own biology and lose twice, once to the external challenge, and again to self-judgment. If we start by calling fear "information," we gain a collaborator. The body can bring energy, focus, and readiness; the mind can bring interpretation, proportion, and purpose. When those two work together, fear returns to its original role- guardian, teacher, and catalyst for timely action.

The Shift from Physical Fear to Psychological Fear-

For most of evolutionary history, fear was short, sharp, and useful. It appeared in the face of an immediate threat, a predator's approach, the sound of thunder, the sight of fire, and disappeared once safety returned. The body's alarm was designed for events, not for ideas. When the danger passed, the system powered down; equilibrium was restored.

Then something extraordinary happened- the human brain grew an imagination. With that gift came language, planning, and creativity, but also a new burden. We could now picture the future before it arrived. We could simulate threats, rehearse loss, and remember failure long after it ended. The mind began to predict danger rather than simply detect it. That single shift turned fear from a biological reflex into a psychological companion.

Inside the brain, the same amygdala that once fired to a snake's movement now fires to a thought about losing a job, a relationship, or reputation. The primitive system cannot distinguish between perceived and imagined threat; it reacts to both with equal seriousness. The body prepares for battle while the battlefield exists only in memory or anticipation. Heart rate rises, muscles tighten, cortisol surges, yet there is nothing tangible to escape.

The modern human therefore lives in a continuous loop- anticipation without resolution. Each scenario the mind constructs creates a pulse of physiological alarm. Because the scenario rarely happens, the system never completes its protective cycle. The body keeps waiting for a finish that never comes. Over time, this incomplete cycle hardens into what we call chronic anxiety.

The problem is not that imagination exists; it is that imagination lacks boundaries. A mind capable of envisioning art, science, and compassion is also capable of envisioning endless catastrophe. Evolution could not have predicted social media, economic volatility, or existential comparison, fields where threat is abstract but constant. The same nervous system that saved our ancestors from predators now responds to inbox alerts and performance reviews with the same chemistry of fear.

Society's response has often been to treat fear as pathology. We label it, medicate it, and try to silence it. Yet the real issue is misapplication, not malfunction. The system is doing its ancient job in a modern world. It is still trying to protect. It just has too much to monitor and too little rest.

Understanding this opens a doorway to compassion. When you feel the familiar tightening in the chest, it is not a personal failure, it is a two-million-year-old intelligence doing what it was built to do. The task is to educate it, not to punish it. When you pause, breathe, and bring awareness to that moment, the higher brain, the prefrontal cortex, reassures the older brain that the danger is imagined, not real. Slowly, repetition builds trust, and the loop begins to loosen.

At its essence, psychological fear is imagination without guidance. Guided imagination becomes foresight, strategy, and creativity; unguided imagination becomes worry. Both use the same neural machinery. The difference lies in awareness, the ability to notice when the mind has slipped from preparation into projection.

From the biological side, fear saved us. From the psychological side, it asks us to grow. The emergence of mental fear was not a cosmic mistake; it was evolution's invitation for consciousness to take its next step, from reaction to reflection, from reflex to reason.

The Cost of Misunderstood Fear-

When the natural intelligence of fear is misunderstood, what once kept humanity safe begins to turn against it. The energy that was designed to sharpen awareness now feeds confusion, exhaustion, and emotional chaos. In the modern age, fear has not disappeared; it has simply changed its disguise. It wears the faces of stress, anger, arrogance, comparison, and chronic busyness.

We live in a world that praises control. Productivity is mistaken for peace, and constant activity for purpose. From childhood we are trained to suppress fear, to appear confident even when uncertain, to smile through pressure, to call anxiety "motivation." Society does not allow space for fear to be understood; it only teaches us to conceal it. But what we suppress never disappears, it migrates. It moves from thought into emotion, from emotion into behavior, from behavior into illness.

Unprocessed fear often reappears as anger. A person who fears rejection may become aggressive to hide vulnerability. Someone who fears failure may become controlling, punishing, or perfectionist. In each case, fear changes costume but not intention; it is still trying to protect. The tragedy is that instead of receiving that message with awareness, we fight it, and by fighting it, we feed it.

The cost of this misunderstanding is visible everywhere. In families, small fears of being unloved grow into endless arguments. In organizations, fear of inadequacy turns into competition and politics. At a societal scale, collective fear, fear of loss, difference, or uncertainty, becomes prejudice and conflict. Beneath every division you can trace the same ancient signal- *protect what feels threatened.*

Technology has amplified the problem. Our ancestors met fear through silence and nature; we meet it through noise and notifications. Every ping, alert, or headline triggers the same neural circuits that once detected predators. The nervous system, flooded by constant stimulus, rarely finds completion. It vibrates in a low-grade state of alarm that we have normalized as "stress."

This chronic activation carries a physical toll. Elevated cortisol disrupts sleep and digestion, weakens immunity, and accelerates cellular aging. The heart works harder; muscles remain partially tense; the brain's default-mode network loops through self-referential worry. Over time, this physiological wear becomes emotional fatigue. People describe it as burnout, but at its core it is misunderstood fear, the body begging for safety that the mind refuses to acknowledge.

There is also a subtler cost- loss of clarity. Fear narrows perception. When threatened, the brain privileges short-term survival over long-term vision. In that tunnel view, creativity collapses, empathy declines, and decision-making becomes reactive. Entire societies have repeated this pattern, frightened minds making fearful choices that sustain the very insecurity they wish to escape.

Yet the most profound loss is spiritual. When fear is mistaken for failure, people lose trust in themselves and in the intelligence of life. They begin to live defensively, guarding against an imagined future. Their attention, which could have been used for wonder, learning, or love, becomes consumed by avoidance. Life becomes smaller, tighter, more mechanical. What was meant to be an instrument of awareness turns into a cage of protection.

Understanding this pattern does not require rejecting progress or technology. It requires remembering their place. The nervous system was not designed for permanent vigilance. The mind was not designed for perpetual comparison. When we interpret every uncertainty as danger, we exhaust the very intelligence that evolution gave us to thrive.

The beginning of healing lies in simple recognition- fear is not proof that something is wrong with you; it is proof that something within you cares. It signals attention, not defect. When acknowledged with honesty, it begins to settle. When suppressed, it grows stronger. The difference between suffering and awareness is not in the amount of fear we feel, but in how deeply we understand its message.

In misunderstanding fear, humanity has created a culture of constant self-defence. In understanding it, we rediscover a culture of connection. Fear was meant to remind us of our fragility so that compassion could emerge. Its original purpose was to unite us in awareness, not separate us in panic.

The cost of misunderstood fear is therefore not only personal but collective. It dims intelligence, erodes health, and fragments society. The correction begins individually, the moment one person pauses, breathes, and listens instead of reacting. That small act of awareness restores the original design. Fear returns to its role as teacher, not tyrant.

The Divine Purpose of Fear-

If we only see fear as a biological reflex or psychological distortion, we miss its higher purpose. Evolution shaped the body to survive, but consciousness shaped fear to awaken. In the grand architecture of life, fear is not an error; it is a sacred signal designed to bring us back to awareness.

When viewed through the spiritual lens, fear performs the most profound of all functions- it exposes our attachment to control. Every fear, whether of loss, death, failure, or rejection, points to something we are trying to hold onto. It is as if the divine intelligence has placed fear as a gentle mirror before the mind, saying,

"Look here, this is where you are still trying to rule life instead of living it."

Fear therefore becomes a teacher of humility. It reminds us that no matter how advanced our logic or how vast our knowledge, there are forces beyond calculation. It invites surrender not as defeat but as recognition, that we are participants in a larger order, not the designers of it.

In the language of the soul, fear is like the gravitational pull that keeps awareness from drifting too far into illusion. When we become intoxicated with certainty or arrogance, fear quietly appears to correct our balance. It is the divine equalizer, ensuring that growth remains anchored in awareness rather than ego.

When we fight fear, we strengthen the ego's illusion of control; when we observe it, we begin to align with divine intelligence. In that observation, the energy of fear transforms. What once felt heavy and suffocating becomes luminous and spacious. You begin to see that the very vibration you once called *fear* is the same energy that, when purified by awareness, becomes alertness, devotion, and love.

This is why the ancient sages never taught people to destroy fear. They taught them to understand it. In the Bhagavad Gita, Krishna tells Arjuna that fear arises from attachment and that freedom is not found by escaping battle but by acting with awareness and surrender. Similarly, in the words of Christ, "Be not afraid" was not a command to suppress fear but a reminder that divine presence renders fear powerless.

When we meditate deeply, we begin to experience this truth directly. The sensations that once signalled fear, tightness in the chest, racing heartbeat, trembling breath, are revealed to be just waves of energy passing through the body. They come and go, but awareness remains untouched. That realization is liberation. You no longer identify with the vibration; you witness it. You no longer say, "I am afraid." You say, "Fear is arising within me." The shift seems small, but it changes everything.

From this space of witnessing, surrender becomes effortless. You stop fighting the current of life. You begin to trust that even what you do not understand is part of divine orchestration. Fear then becomes an ally, a way the universe ensures that you remember the truth of your own impermanence and dependence on the greater whole.

It is also worth recognizing that fear deepens love. Without the awareness of loss, we would not cherish connection. Without the awareness of impermanence, we would not value the moment. In this sense, fear is the contrast that allows love and faith to exist. It shapes compassion, patience, and empathy, all qualities that evolve only when the heart has known vulnerability.

At the deepest level, the divine uses fear to call us inward. When fear becomes unbearable, it drives us to question everything, our motives, our attachments, our very identity. This questioning is not punishment; it is the beginning of awakening. Fear dismantles the false so that the real can be seen. It strips away the illusion of control and exposes the eternal stillness behind all movement.

That stillness is God's signature within us, the untouched awareness that no fear can corrupt. Once you taste that silence, fear loses its authority. It may visit, but it no longer governs. You meet it like an old friend who once frightened you but now reminds you how far you've come.

From this understanding arises reverence. We begin to thank fear instead of rejecting it. We realize that every moment of trembling was a whisper from the divine, saying,

"Wake up. You are not this body. You are not this mind. You are the awareness that sees both."

Fear's divine purpose, then, is nothing less than awakening. It pushes the finite self to discover the infinite. It breaks the arrogance of control so that surrender can blossom. It tests the limits of trust so that faith can become real. When understood deeply, fear becomes the most sacred threshold in human experience, the point where survival ends and awakening begins.

The New Understanding-

The journey through fear, from instinct to imagination and finally to awareness, brings us to a new understanding, one that integrates science, psychology, and spirit into a single truth fear is not the enemy of peace; misunderstanding is.

Every form of fear, physical, emotional, or existential, belongs to a continuum of intelligence. At its base, it preserves life. In its distorted form, it limits life. And in its highest form, it awakens life. The goal, therefore, is not to escape fear but to evolve through it.

To understand this new relationship, we must first see that fear is energy, not emotion. Energy itself is neutral; it gains meaning from interpretation. The same vibration that fuels anxiety can also fuel courage. The same restlessness that causes worry can, when understood, become alertness. What transforms fear is not suppression, but awareness.

From Resistance to Relationship-

When we resist fear, we divide ourselves. The mind begins a battle it cannot win- one part of us tries to eliminate what another part of us naturally produces. This inner conflict drains energy, attention, and creativity. But when we stop fighting and start listening, the war ends. Fear becomes part of the conversation rather than the opponent.

Imagine two voices within you- the instinct that says "Be careful" and the awareness that says "Be present." When they speak together, wisdom emerges. When they argue, anxiety grows. The new understanding is not about silencing either voice but about letting awareness lead the dialogue.

Awareness transforms fear by revealing its purpose. You begin to ask- What is this energy trying to tell me? Sometimes the answer is practical, rest, slow down, prepare. Sometimes it is existential, let go, trust, surrender. Fear's message always points toward alignment.

The Practice of Observation-

The practice begins with simple observation. The next time fear arises, do not label it as "bad." Notice how it feels in the body, the tightening, the pulse, the thought that follows. Then remind yourself- "This is energy moving." Stay with it without judging. In a few moments, you will notice a subtle gap between the observer and the observed. That gap is freedom.

Repeated often, this practice rewires the relationship between the amygdala and the prefrontal cortex, the emotional and reasoning centers of the brain. The system learns that fear can be experienced safely. Physiologically, recovery quickens; psychologically, resilience grows; spiritually, you begin to see that awareness is untouched by any emotion passing through it.

Integrating the Three Dimensions-

Fear exists on three levels of intelligence, biological, psychological, and divine, and each serves a distinct purpose in the evolution of awareness. At the biological level, fear ensures survival. It sharpens the senses, mobilizes the body, and prepares us to face what could endanger life. At the psychological level, it becomes the mirror of self-knowledge. It reveals where we are attached, what we value, and what we still misunderstand about ourselves. At the divine level, fear transforms into guidance. It begins to point beyond the mind, beyond control, toward surrender, the state where we recognize that life itself is the protector, not merely the one being protected.

These are not separate realities but stages of one continuous awakening. In the beginning, fear helps us live. Later, it teaches us to understand. Eventually, it invites us to trust. Most people spend their lives oscillating between the first two, survival and struggle , never realizing that both are meant to lead to the third: surrender.

When you begin to see fear through this integrated awareness, something subtle changes. Fear no longer appears as an obstacle but as a messenger. Each time it arises, you can sense a pattern , fear before growth, fear before clarity, fear before truth. You stop asking, "Why is this happening to me?" and start asking, "What is this trying to reveal?" That single change of question turns turmoil into teaching.

Living Without Fear-

To live without fear does not mean never feeling afraid. It means no longer being ruled by fear's voice. A fearless life is not careless; it is conscious. You move with awareness instead of compulsion. You respond instead of reacting.

Fear will still appear, but its nature changes. It no longer commands you , it communicates with you. When it visits, you recognize it as an old companion, sometimes intense, sometimes inconvenient, but never malicious. You listen, you breathe, and you thank it for reminding you to stay awake.

This is the quiet strength of conscious living. You become capable of walking through uncertainty without losing balance. Decisions come from clarity, not panic. You begin to live, not defensively, but deliberately , not trying to avoid pain, but trusting yourself to move through it with grace.

From Fear to Gratitude-

The deepest transformation happens when understanding turns into gratitude. You begin to see that fear was never an enemy, it was an ancient intelligence, walking beside you since the beginning, keeping you alert to life's fragility and value. What once felt like tension now feels like tenderness. You realize fear was not there to punish you for being human; it was there to protect your humanity.

Gratitude changes the vibration of fear. It converts contraction into expansion. The body relaxes, the breath slows, and the mind regains its natural clarity. When you no longer fight your inner experience, it begins to cooperate. That is when joy returns , not the restless joy of escape, but the serene joy of understanding.

You see, life's intelligence has never worked against you. It only disguises its lessons in the language of discomfort so that awareness can grow. Every fear you have faced has been a doorway into a wider peace. Every struggle has been an invitation to know yourself more deeply.

The Essence of the New Understanding-

At last, fear reveals its final gift: awakening. It was never sent to break you; it was sent to awaken the deeper strength already within you. Every tremor of anxiety, every shadow of uncertainty, every moment of hesitation was life asking you to remember, that you are more than your reactions, more than your thoughts, more than your fears.

In this new understanding, fear and love are no longer opposites. They are movements of the same sacred energy, different notes of one song. Fear teaches reverence; love teaches expansion. Together they sustain the rhythm of life.

You begin to see existence not as divided between light and dark, gain and loss, comfort and pain , but as one continuous movement of intelligence. Every experience carries a message, every feeling has meaning. Nothing is against you; everything is speaking to you.

And when this realization becomes steady, the purpose of fear is complete. It no longer needs to shout for your attention , because awareness has already heard.

Fear as Energy, Not Emotion-

Most people speak of fear as if it were a feeling, something we have. In truth, fear is not a fixed emotion; it is a movement of energy passing through awareness. Emotion is simply how the mind interprets that movement. Understanding this subtle distinction changes everything.

When fear arises, what actually happens first is energy activation. The body detects a perceived threat and releases stored potential- electrical impulses race through neurons, hormones surge into the bloodstream, and the entire field of attention contracts around one point. Before a single thought forms, a wave of energy has already moved. The mind then interprets that wave, naming it fear, anxiety, or tension, based on memory and meaning.

Seen in this light, fear is neutral. It is the same life-force that powers inspiration and creativity, only vibrating at a higher frequency and directed toward protection rather than expression. The trembling before a performance, the pulse before an exam, the sudden stillness before danger, each is raw energy seeking direction.

The Physics of Emotion-

Energy cannot be destroyed; it only changes form. The same law applies to inner experience. When we resist fear, we block that energy. Blocked energy does not disappear, it stagnates. It turns into heaviness, confusion, or fatigue. When we allow it to move with awareness, it transforms into clarity, focus, and vitality. This is why deep breathing, movement, or meditation can dissolve anxiety without a single logical argument- they restore flow where resistance created friction.

Fear, then, is not asking to be removed but released. It needs motion, not suppression. The moment you allow the sensation to exist without naming it, the energy begins to reorganize itself. Awareness acts as the conductor, guiding the current toward balance.

From Emotion to Energy Awareness-

Modern psychology often treats fear as a cognitive problem, something to be reasoned with or reprogrammed. But reasoning can only work within thought; energy lies beneath it. True transformation begins when you sense fear as vibration, not story.

Close your eyes for a moment and observe a recent memory of fear. Notice where it lives in the body- chest, stomach, throat. Instead of analyzing *why* it's there, simply feel its texture, tight, warm, restless. Stay still until the wave completes itself. You will sense a shift- the same current that felt threatening begins to feel alive. This is energy turning back into awareness.

Over time, you learn to recognize every emotional disturbance as a form of this energy trying to return home. Anger is compressed vitality; sadness is slowed tenderness; fear is alertness seeking alignment. Once you see this pattern, you no longer categorize experiences as positive or negative. You see them as movements of consciousness, each with its own frequency and lesson.

The Role of Awareness-

Awareness does not fight energy; it witnesses it into balance. The mind's habit is to interfere, to judge, analyze, or suppress. Awareness simply watches. That watching itself is the highest healing. The instant you observe fear without story, you create space between the observer and the observed. In that space, energy can move freely. What once felt like threat now becomes pure life-force.

This is why meditative traditions emphasize observation without reaction. Breath, stillness, and presence are not escape mechanisms; they are tuning forks. They align human vibration with the deeper rhythm of existence. When aligned, fear no longer feels like contraction; it feels like awakening, a reminder that you are alive, alert, and connected.

Energy Transmutation-

As understanding deepens, fear evolves through three recognizable stages-

1. Resistance – energy trapped as tension.
2. Recognition – awareness noticing the movement.
3. Transmutation – the same energy becoming clarity and strength.

In transmutation, nothing is lost. The electricity of fear becomes the luminosity of awareness. The same surge that once triggered panic now fuels insight. This is why people often report that their greatest breakthroughs arrive after their deepest fears. The energy released by surrender becomes creativity, compassion, and intuition.

A Living Practice-

To live this truth, one must practice gentle awareness throughout daily life. When a difficult situation arises, pause before reacting. Feel the surge of energy rather than the narrative. Let it move through you. Speak or act only when the body softens again. With repetition, the nervous system learns trust; the old reflex to contract gives way to a new reflex to observe.

This is the beginning of energetic mastery, not control, but cooperation. You no longer fear because you recognize it as the same current that animates breath, thought, and movement. The current itself is innocent. It only becomes painful when resisted.

Why Fear Cannot Be Erased, Only Transformed-

Every attempt to erase fear begins with a misunderstanding of its nature. People want freedom from fear as if fear were a stain on consciousness, something that can be removed with enough effort, success, or meditation. But fear is not an intruder in the mind; it is an expression of life itself. You can no more erase fear than you can erase movement, sensation, or thought. You can only transform your relationship with it.

The Illusion of Eradication-

For centuries, humans have tried to conquer fear through domination, wealth, control, power, or rigid belief. Yet, the more we build walls against fear, the more subtly it returns. We fear losing what we built to escape it. This is the paradox- resistance multiplies the very thing we wish to remove. Fear cannot be suppressed or destroyed because it arises from the same source as love, curiosity, and awareness, the movement of energy through consciousness. To erase fear would mean to erase sensitivity itself.

The absence of fear is not courage; it is numbness. A mind without any fear would not protect the body, cherish relationships, or value existence. Fear gives meaning to care. It reminds us that what we love can be lost and therefore must be honoured. To want to eliminate fear completely is to wish for a sterile life, safe perhaps, but lifeless.

The Natural Cycle of Transformation-

Like fire, fear is neither good nor bad; its impact depends on how it is handled. Fire can destroy or illuminate. Fear can imprison or awaken. Transformation begins when you stop asking, "How do I get rid of fear?" and start asking, "What is fear trying to show me?" The question changes the chemistry of the mind. What was once a command becomes curiosity. And curiosity invites light.

The process of transformation follows a natural rhythm-

1. Recognition, Becoming aware that fear is present, without denial.
2. Acceptance, Allowing the sensation to exist without judgment or urgency.
3. Understanding, Seeing the pattern that created it- attachment, uncertainty, or control.
4. Integration, Using the energy of fear as guidance rather than opposition.

In this rhythm, fear completes its cycle. What once felt like pressure becomes movement; what felt like darkness becomes depth. The energy doesn't disappear; it evolves.

Fear as a Messenger of Change-

Every fear carries information. Fear of failure signals the need for clarity of purpose. Fear of loss reveals where attachment still binds the heart. Fear of rejection points toward the need for self-acceptance. Fear of death whispers of impermanence and humility. When we listen without panic, each fear becomes a teacher with a message- "Look where you have mistaken the temporary for the eternal."

When this insight dawns, the relationship with fear becomes sacred. You begin to see that it never sought to harm you, only to wake you. Like a strict teacher, fear raises its voice when you ignore its lesson, then softens when you understand. Transformation happens not by fighting the teacher but by learning what it was trying to say.

The Energy of Continuity-

Biologically, fear is hardwired. It cannot be erased because it serves the continuity of life. Spiritually, fear persists because it serves the continuity of awareness. Both are forms of intelligence- one protects the body, the other refines the soul. The divine design is perfect in its symmetry. Just as muscles grow stronger through resistance, awareness expands through fear. Without challenge, consciousness would remain dormant. Each wave of fear is an invitation to remember the eternal strength behind the temporary form.

The Shift of Identity-

When fear feels unbearable, it is not the energy that hurts but our identification with it. We believe we are the fear. We forget that we are the awareness in which fear arises. The transformation, therefore, is not about removing fear but about remembering identity. The ocean does not resist the waves; it knows they belong to it. In the same way, awareness does not resist emotions; it recognizes them as movements within itself. When you rest as awareness, fear becomes one of many ripples on the surface of your vast stillness.

This realization dissolves the illusion of control. You stop expecting a life without storms and begin cultivating the strength to remain still within them. The mature mind does not pray for calm seas; it learns to sail. That is transformation.

The Freedom Beyond Erasure-

Freedom from fear is not the absence of fear but the absence of dependence on it. When fear no longer dictates your choices, you are free. When its arrival no longer terrifies you, you are wise. When its energy becomes your alertness instead of your prison, you are awake.

Fear will visit you again and again, before change, before growth, before revelation, but each visit will feel different. The same current that once burned now illuminates. The same thought that once paralyzed now reminds you of life's preciousness. In that moment, you realize that fear has fulfilled its purpose- it has transformed from resistance into reverence.

The Essence-

Fear cannot be erased because it was never separate from you. It is the trembling edge of life reminding you that you are alive. It is the pulse of awareness testing its own strength. When you stop demanding its absence and start embracing its intelligence, it changes form, from contraction to clarity, from protection to participation, from human to divine.

Transformation, therefore, is not an event but a relationship, the ongoing dialogue between energy and awareness. The goal is not silence, but harmony.

In the end, you do not conquer fear.
You become transparent to it.
It moves through you like wind through open space, present, powerful, but unable to disturb the stillness it passes through.

2 THE ARCHITECTURE OF THE MIND

How Thoughts, Memory, and Imagination Create Fear-

Fear is not born in the world around us but in the mind's interpretation of it. The external event, an unexpected noise, a disapproving glance, a message left unanswered, is neutral until thought assigns it meaning. That meaning is constructed through three forces that shape all inner experience- thought, memory, and imagination.

The Loop of Thought-

Thought is the mind's tool for navigation. It allows us to compare, predict, and plan. But the same mechanism that gives us order also creates distortion. Thought never deals with reality directly; it deals with symbols of reality, words, images, judgments. When a sound startles you, it lasts only a second. When thought enters, it continues for hours- "What if something is wrong? What if it happens again?" The mind turns a moment into a story. Fear is not in the sound; it is in the story.

Thought thrives on continuity. It does not know how to stop. Each fearful thought creates another to justify itself, forming a self-sustaining chain. This loop gives fear its persistence. The event ends, but the story remains alive through repetition. The mind replays it, each time strengthening the emotional trace.

The Weight of Memory-

Memory is the archive that thought uses to interpret the present. It is not passive storage; it is active shaping. Every experience leaves an imprint, a neural pattern encoded with emotion. When the present resembles a past moment of pain, memory revives the old pattern and colors perception. A harsh tone in a meeting may echo the voice of a critical parent; a delay in response may resurrect the loneliness of childhood rejection. The mind doesn't distinguish between then and now, it simply reacts to familiar frequency. Fear is often not about the current event but about the memory it awakens.

This is why two people can experience the same situation and feel entirely different emotions. One sees danger; another sees opportunity. The difference lies not in reality but in the memory filtering it.

Memory's function is protective- it warns, "Last time you touched fire, it burned." But it also overextends its reach. It warns even when the fire is gone. In this way, fear becomes habitual, a reflex conditioned by past pain rather than current risk.

The Theater of Imagination-

If thought creates the story and memory provides the script, imagination builds the stage. It extends fear into time. The mind projects what might happen and lives it as though it were happening now. A simple uncertainty, "Will I lose my job?", turns into vivid internal cinema- the conversation, the disappointment, the loss of respect, the inability to recover. Each image triggers the same biochemical reactions as a real event. The body sweats, heart rate rises, muscles tighten. The imagined danger feels authentic because the nervous system cannot tell the difference between mental picture and sensory reality.

Imagination is one of humanity's greatest powers. It creates art, innovation, and empathy. Yet when directed by fear, it becomes self-torture. The future becomes an emotional hologram, a place the body suffers before the mind arrives.

The Fear Triangle-

These three forces, thought, memory, and imagination, form what we can call the Fear Triangle. Thought links the past and future; memory supplies emotional charge; imagination extends duration. Together they build a reality that feels solid, even though it exists entirely in consciousness.

This structure is why fear seems unshakable- it is reinforced from multiple sides. Thought says, "This could happen." Memory says, "It happened before." Imagination says, "It's happening again." And awareness, if unconscious, believes them all.

Breaking the triangle requires awareness. When you watch thought without joining it, recall memory without identifying with it, and allow imagination without believing it, the structure collapses. What remains is sensation, pure energy without narrative. In that space, fear loses its power because it has lost its storyteller.

From Mental Mechanics to Inner Freedom-

Understanding how the mind constructs fear allows compassion to replace frustration. You realize that the mind is not malicious; it is mechanical. It repeats what it knows. It fears what it cannot predict. Awareness brings flexibility, the ability to respond freshly rather than react habitually.

The purpose of spiritual or meditative practice is not to stop thought, erase memory, or silence imagination, but to reclaim authorship. You stop letting these faculties create fear unconsciously and begin using them consciously for creation, reflection, and wisdom. Thought becomes clear reasoning, memory becomes learning, imagination becomes vision. Fear transforms into insight.

The moment you see the machinery, you step outside it.
You realize- the mind produces fear, but awareness does not.
And in that realization lies the beginning of true freedom.

The Silent Mechanics of Fear-

Fear is not an illusion; it is a real biological process designed to protect life. Deep within the human brain exists a set of intelligent mechanisms that have evolved over millions of years to detect threat, respond instantly, and preserve survival. These mechanisms, tiny in size but vast in influence, operate so quickly that they often react before conscious thought even begins.

When a person senses danger, the brain's internal network lights up in an intricate sequence. One part of this network functions like an alarm, scanning for potential harm and signaling the body to prepare for action. Another part acts like a memory bank, comparing the current situation with past experiences to assess whether the threat is familiar. A third region serves as a rational controller, evaluating whether the alarm is justified and deciding what action, if any, needs to be taken.

In a balanced state, these three functions operate in harmony. The alarm warns, the memory verifies, and the reason decides. Together, they create a sense of alertness that helps a person respond to challenges effectively. This is the intelligence of fear, the reason humanity survived countless natural dangers long before civilization existed.

However, in modern life, the same ancient system has become overstimulated. The brain still reacts as if every uncertainty were a threat to physical survival. A message from a supervisor, a delay in response, or a thought about the future can trigger the same chemical cascade as a predator once did. The result is a physiological response, rapid heartbeat, shallow breathing, muscle tension, that feels real even though the danger exists only in the imagination.

When these signals repeat too often, they strengthen the brain's wiring. The body begins to associate ordinary experiences with danger, and fear becomes habitual. The alarm grows louder, the memory keeps replaying, and the rational mind loses control. The person starts living in a continuous loop of alertness, unable to relax even in moments of safety.

Yet, the same system that creates fear also holds the key to transformation. The human brain is not a fixed machine, it is adaptive, fluid, and constantly learning. Neuroscience calls this neuroplasticity- the ability of the brain to reorganize itself by forming new connections. Every time a person responds to fear with awareness instead of resistance, new neural pathways are created. The body learns that calm is also safe, not only panic.

When one observes a fearful moment consciously, without judgment or avoidance, the internal chemistry begins to shift. Stress hormones like cortisol gradually reduce, and neurotransmitters such as serotonin and dopamine restore balance. The alarm system becomes less reactive, memory becomes more accurate, and rational clarity returns. Awareness itself becomes the teacher that re-educates the brain.

In simple terms, fear is not an enemy to be removed but a signal to be understood. It shows where the mind is still conditioned to react rather than respond. When awareness grows, the relationship with fear changes from hostility to cooperation. The same mechanism that once caused distress becomes a source of alertness, strength, and sensitivity.

Ultimately, the architecture of the mind is not flawed, it is misunderstood. Fear was never designed to punish or paralyze; it was meant to protect. When we learn to use its intelligence consciously, it stops being a barrier and becomes a guide. It tells us where to pay attention, when to pause, and how to grow.

Fear, therefore, is not a defect in the human system but a doorway to a higher form of awareness. The key is not to silence the alarm but to understand what it's trying to say.

How Awareness Alters Brain Chemistry-

The human brain is a living field of communication. Every thought, emotion, and breath sends ripples through this field, shaping the way neurons connect and signals travel. What we repeatedly think and feel becomes the brain's habitual language. Over time, the chemistry of the mind begins to mirror the chemistry of our inner state.

Fear, anxiety, and chronic stress are not only emotional experiences; they are also biological patterns. When the body perceives threat, real or imagined, the brain releases specific chemicals such as adrenaline and cortisol. These hormones sharpen attention and prepare the body for action, but when they circulate too often, they create exhaustion, irritability, and a persistent sense of tension. The nervous system remains in a state of alert, unable to rest or regenerate.

Awareness changes this chemistry from within. It does not stop hormones directly; it changes the *message* that the brain receives. When a person becomes consciously aware of their thoughts, feelings, and bodily sensations without reacting, the brain interprets that state as safety. This single recognition, *I am aware and still breathing*, sends a signal to deactivate the alarm circuits. The stress response begins to ease, and the body's restorative systems quietly reawaken.

Over time, this practice of awareness creates measurable biological effects. Functional MRI studies show that regular meditation and mindful observation reduce activity in the brain's fear centers while increasing activity in regions responsible for calm and reasoning. The pathways between the emotional and rational parts of the brain strengthen, allowing them to communicate more efficiently. As a result, fear loses its ability to dominate the mind.

Neurochemically, awareness triggers a shift from stress hormones to stabilizing neurotransmitters such as serotonin, GABA, and dopamine. These substances do not merely make one "feel good"; they restore balance, improve clarity, and enhance the capacity to think clearly under pressure. Awareness, therefore, is not passive; it is biologically active. It rewires the neural landscape through direct experience, not belief.

One of the most profound aspects of awareness is that it integrates both mind and body. When attention rests on the breath, the heartbeat, or the present moment, the parasympathetic nervous system, the body's natural relaxation response, activates automatically. Heart rate slows, blood pressure normalizes, and the immune system strengthens. The same body that once trembled under fear now learns calmness as its new default state.

This transformation does not happen through force or positive thinking. It happens through simple observation without resistance. The mind's habitual reactions lose strength each time they are seen clearly. Awareness does not fight the old patterns; it replaces them with understanding. When the mind watches itself without judgment, it sends a message deeper than thought- All is well; there is no danger here. That message, repeated gently through daily awareness, reprograms the entire biological system toward stability.

Over months or even weeks, people who practice awareness consistently begin to feel changes that are both emotional and physical. Sleep improves, concentration deepens, and emotional reactivity lessens. These changes are not abstract, they are neurochemical confirmations that the body is learning peace.

At the spiritual level, this is the same principle ancient masters spoke of when they described meditation as purification. What they called *purity of mind* is, in modern language, the restoration of healthy brain chemistry. The patterns of tension and overreaction dissolve, and what remains is a clear, balanced system aligned with the rhythm of life.

In essence, awareness does not add something new to the brain; it restores its natural order. It reminds the nervous system that safety is the truth of existence, not danger. Through repeated awareness, the brain's chemistry begins to express that truth, calmly, steadily, and naturally. Fear no longer commands; it simply signals. Awareness listens, responds, and continues to evolve.

When awareness becomes the constant background of life, the human brain no longer oscillates between panic and relief. It rests in an intelligent equilibrium, alert yet peaceful, active yet still. In this state, the same brain that once created fear becomes the instrument through which consciousness experiences freedom.

---

3 THE INVISIBLE COMMUNITY OF THE FEARFUL

Hidden Fear-

Fear today does not often shout. It hides, beneath the surface of ambition, productivity, and planning. In the ancient world, fear made people run. In the modern world, it makes them move endlessly. We overthink, overwork, and over plan, calling it discipline or success. But underneath the motion lies the same old trembling: What if I am not enough? What if things fall apart when I stop?

When the mind cannot sit still, it is rarely because it is too intelligent, it is because it is frightened. Overthinking is not deeper thought; it is thought in captivity. The mind circles the same ideas again and again, hoping that one more round of analysis will erase uncertainty. Fear disguises itself as logic, as preparation, as care. But its hidden motive is control.

Overworking follows the same pattern in motion. Society applauds it, the full calendar, the endless emails, the late-night glow of screens. Yet what looks like dedication is often desperation. The mind whispers, If I stop, something will go wrong. The body obeys, pushing beyond exhaustion, mistaking movement for safety. We call it commitment, but it is fear wearing a professional mask.

Then comes overplanning, the most respectable disguise of all. The planner believes that if everything is mapped perfectly, nothing will hurt. But plans are only stories about the future, not promises. Life has never signed the agreement. When the unknown arrives, as it always does, the carefully built structure collapses into anxiety.

These patterns have one root: the wish to make life permanent. We build routines and systems, not merely to organize time, but to shield ourselves from its unpredictability. Yet the universe itself moves by change. When we try to make it still, we end up trembling before its natural flow.

The Illusion of Control and Permanence-

The great paradox of human life is that we trust technology more than time, but time always wins. At the heart of nearly every fear is a quiet bargain: If I can control enough variables, I will be safe. The mind believes that control brings peace. It plans, predicts, and protects. But the more we grip, the more fragile everything becomes.

Control begins with good intention. The mind simply wants stability, the same way the body seeks balance. But stability is not the same as stillness. Everything in nature flows, day and night, seasons, tides, even breath. Permanence is not part of life's design; rhythm is.

Yet the modern mind resists that rhythm. It chases permanence, hoping that success, love, or status will freeze into eternity. It resists endings and worships guarantees. And when change inevitably comes, fear awakens. What we call "fear of loss" is often fear of impermanence, the refusal to accept that all things, by nature, move.

The more we try to control life, the more anxious we become. Every plan opens another question: What if it fails? Every success breeds the next worry: Can I keep it? The control we seek multiplies the uncertainty we fear.

Awareness changes this relationship. When we begin to see that control has limits, and that those limits are not threats but truths, peace returns. Control governs the outer world; trust governs the inner one. Once you stop demanding guarantees, life stops feeling like a test.

True stability is not the absence of change; it is the ability to remain steady within it. The wise do not grip the river; they learn to swim with it. Control comforts for a moment, but surrender frees for a lifetime.

When Stability Becomes Anxiety-

All human beings long for stability. It is natural. We want life to be predictable, safe, and gentle. But when that desire hardens into a demand, life must not change, anxiety begins.

Anxiety is born not from uncertainty itself, but from our resistance to it. The mind wants to live in a universe where everything obeys its plans. But the real universe is alive, expanding, shifting, creating. When we insist that it should freeze in place, we create tension against reality itself.

Modern society magnifies this. It teaches that stability is measured by income, reputation, or relationships. These are valuable, but temporary. When identity attaches to them, even small tremors, a delay, a disagreement, a market dip, feel like existential threats. The fear is not about the event; it is about the imagined collapse of stability.

That is why people overthink, overwork, and overprepare, not because they crave perfection, but because they fear collapse. The nervous system mistakes unpredictability for danger and keeps the body in constant alert. Over time, this vigilance drains energy, joy, and creativity. Burnout is not fatigue, it is fear that has stayed too long.

The antidote is not control, but consciousness. True stability comes not from holding life still, but from knowing you can stay still while life moves. Awareness teaches this difference. When your peace no longer depends on conditions, you are free.

Paradoxically, the more we chase stability, the less stable we feel. The more we cling, the more fragile life appears. But when you release the demand for control, trust quietly takes its place. You begin to see uncertainty not as danger, but as movement, the pulse of a living universe.

Anxiety fades, not because everything becomes predictable, but because you stop insisting that it must be. Peace is not found in the stillness of circumstances, but in the stillness of being.

The Quiet Realization-

When awareness deepens, you begin to see how much of human life is shaped by hidden fear. The endless activity, the striving for order, the restless search for certainty, all expressions of the same ancient instinct trying to adapt to a complex age.

But now you understand something the early humans did not: fear is not the only intelligence within you. There is another, awareness, capable of seeing fear without being trapped by it. When the two meet, fear softens. It loses its disguise and returns to its rightful role, not as master, but as messenger.

Then, even in the busiest moments of modern life, you remain free.

4 THE LAW OF CHANGE

The Cosmic Rule of Impermanence-

If there is one law that governs every atom, every life, and every emotion, it is the law of change. Nothing in existence stands still. The stars expand and collapse, rivers shift their course, cells renew, and thoughts rise and dissolve. Life does not resist movement; it *is* movement. Impermanence is not an interruption in the pattern, it is the pattern itself.

Human beings, however, live as if they were exceptions to this law. We build homes, relationships, and identities with the unconscious hope that they will remain exactly as they are. We cling to what is pleasant, resist what is painful, and call that control. Yet nature has never promised permanence; it has only promised continuity through transformation. What appears to end is always becoming something else.

This is the same rhythm that beats through the cosmos. Stars are born, burn, and fade into dust, and that dust becomes the soil of new creation. Seasons turn, not because they choose to, but because they must. Every dawn carries the memory of darkness, and every dusk carries the promise of light. Existence moves like breath, in and out, expansion and release, a perfect balance between creation and dissolution.

The human mind, in contrast, seeks stillness not as peace but as preservation. It wants the good moments to last forever and the difficult ones to end instantly. It forgets that both are made of the same fabric of time. To demand permanence in a world built on impermanence is to struggle against the very flow that sustains life.

Ancient wisdom traditions recognized this long before modern science began to measure it. They taught that attachment to the unchanging is the root of suffering, while acceptance of change is liberation. When we align with impermanence, life stops feeling like a battle and begins to feel like a dance, a continuous exchange between holding and letting go.

Even our emotions follow this cosmic rhythm. Joy, sadness, love, fear, none of them stay. They arise, express, and dissolve. The problem is not that emotions change; the problem is that the mind insists they shouldn't (struggle to control them). We call it emotional instability, but in truth, it is emotional nature. Just as waves are the movement of the ocean, feelings are the movement of consciousness. They are meant to rise and fall.

Understanding impermanence is not an invitation to detachment or indifference. It is an invitation to presence. When we accept that nothing lasts, every moment becomes infinitely valuable. Love is deeper when we know it will pass; joy is purer when we stop trying to hold it; even pain becomes meaningful when we see it as transition, not punishment.

Impermanence is not a flaw in creation, it is its intelligence. Without it, there would be no renewal, no growth, no possibility. A world without impermanence would be a world without evolution, without movement, without life.

When awareness matures, one begins to sense the elegance of this law. You watch your thoughts change, your body change, your roles change, and instead of feeling loss, you begin to see the pattern behind it all. You recognize that you are not the changing forms but the unchanging witness through which change is seen. The river flows, but the awareness that observes the river remains still.

To live with this understanding is to live in harmony with the cosmos. You no longer fight against endings, because you see that every ending is preparation for a beginning. You no longer fear uncertainty, because you see that the unknown is simply the next chapter of what you already are. Impermanence, once feared as loss, becomes a teacher, reminding you that the only thing eternal is transformation itself.

Why Resistance to Change Creates Suffering-

Change by itself never causes pain; resistance does. What hurts is not the movement of life but the mind's refusal to move with it. When something shifts, a relationship ends, a job evolves, an identity dissolves, the event itself is neutral. It is part of the natural cycle through which existence renews itself. Suffering begins the moment the mind says, "This should not have happened."

The human brain seeks predictability because it equates familiarity with safety. When something changes, even for the better, the nervous system perceives uncertainty as risk. It does not see transformation; it senses danger. In that instant, fear arises, not because the future is harmful, but because it is unknown. The body tightens, thought races, and emotion follows. Thus, resistance begins as a form of self-protection, but it soon turns into self-inflicted pain.

The paradox is that everything we cherish in life, love, growth, discovery, comes only through change. Without change, no flower would bloom, no child would grow, no wisdom would mature. Yet, the very process that brings renewal is the one we resist the most. We want progress without discomfort, evolution without uncertainty, and renewal without release. Life, however, does not work through avoidance; it works through movement.

When resistance takes root, suffering expands. The mind keeps replaying the past, trying to restore what once was. It clings to memory as though memory could recreate reality. But the more it clings, the more life slips forward, pulling everything familiar away. This tug-of-war between "what is" and "what was" becomes the essence of suffering. The stronger the attachment, the deeper the pain.

Awareness begins where resistance ends. The moment you stop fighting change, energy that was trapped in struggle becomes available for understanding. You begin to see that every ending carries the seed of a beginning, that loss is not destruction but transformation. Acceptance does not mean passive submission; it means recognizing that life moves with or without your permission, and choosing to move consciously with it.

Resistance also distorts perception. When the mind is unwilling to accept change, it magnifies the negative and overlooks the opportunity hidden within transition. It focuses on what has been taken rather than what is being offered. But when awareness expands, perception reverses- the same event that once seemed catastrophic begins to reveal meaning. Pain becomes purification; endings become initiation.

Spiritual traditions often describe this moment as surrender, not a surrender to fate, but a surrender of illusion. The illusion is that we can stop impermanence through effort, control, or prayer. True surrender is not defeat; it is cooperation with the deeper intelligence of life. When we stop resisting, we begin to see that life was never against us; it was always guiding us to outgrow our old forms.

Every transformation demands space. Something must dissolve for something new to take shape. The falling of leaves makes room for spring; the silence after loss allows reflection; the uncertainty after change opens the field for discovery. What feels like emptiness is often preparation. The moment you stop resisting, what looked like an ending reveals itself as evolution.

Suffering ends not because change stops, but because resistance loses meaning. You start seeing life as a conversation between the known and the unknown, between what you are now and what you are becoming. When that realization settles, fear loses its foundation. You no longer demand that life obey your plan; instead, you participate in its rhythm.

To resist change is to fight the universe. To accept it is to become part of its intelligence. One path leads to exhaustion; the other to peace. And the most remarkable truth is this- the moment you stop resisting, change no longer feels like loss, it feels like movement, like breathing, like life doing what it has always done, evolving through you.

Living in Alignment with Universal Rhythm-

To live in alignment with the rhythm of the universe is to live without inner conflict. It does not mean that life will always be comfortable or predictable, but that the mind will no longer fight what comes and goes. This alignment is not about achieving balance once; it is about recognizing that balance itself is movement, a continuous flow between holding on and letting go, acting and resting, rising and falling.

The universe moves in cycles, and everything within it follows that rhythm, the tides, the seasons, the heartbeat, the breath. Expansion and contraction are the twin movements through which creation expresses itself. When we breathe in, we gather; when we breathe out, we release. The same principle governs emotions, relationships, and circumstances. To live consciously is to sense this rhythm within ourselves and act in harmony with it.

Most people suffer not because life moves too fast, but because they move out of sync with its flow. They cling when it is time to release or withdraw when it is time to act. They try to hold summer in the middle of winter. This resistance creates friction, the subtle anxiety of being out of tune with life's natural order. The remedy is not control but attunement- learning to listen, to sense when to move forward and when to pause, when to speak and when to stay silent.

Living in alignment with the universal rhythm begins with awareness. Awareness allows us to see change as communication, not disruption. Every shift in life, whether external or internal, is a message from existence, guiding us toward evolution. The more aware we become, the more clearly we recognize this pattern. A closed door does not mean rejection; it may mean redirection. A delay does not mean denial; it often means preparation. Life rarely makes mistakes, it simply moves in ways that our limited vision cannot yet comprehend.

When awareness deepens, acceptance follows naturally. Acceptance is not passivity; it is intelligent cooperation. It is the willingness to say, "If life is changing, there must be a reason, let me move with it, not against it." Such acceptance brings a deep relaxation that no external achievement can provide. The nervous system calms, the mind becomes quiet, and intuition begins to surface. You start feeling life's timing rather than forcing your own.

In this state, action becomes effortless. You still plan, work, and create, but from a place of flow rather than fear. When an idea arrives, you act with full energy; when it fades, you rest without guilt. You understand that both movement and stillness are expressions of the same intelligence. The wise live this way, they participate in life's unfolding without trying to rewrite its script.

Living in rhythm also means embracing uncertainty. The unknown is not an error in the design of existence; it is its essential element. The next breath, the next hour, the next year, all remain unseen so that life can remain alive. If everything were certain, there would be no creativity, no discovery, no wonder. To align with the universe is to trust this uncertainty as the space where possibilities are born.

Gradually, this trust becomes natural. You stop dividing life into good and bad, gain and loss, success and failure. You begin to see them as waves in the same ocean, each one carrying you further into understanding. When you live this way, gratitude replaces anxiety. You thank life not only for what it gives but also for what it takes away, because you see that both are acts of guidance.

Ultimately, alignment with universal rhythm is not something to achieve, it is something to remember. Deep within, you are already part of that rhythm. Your breath, your heartbeat, your awareness, all follow the same pulse that moves stars and galaxies. The more you trust this truth, the lighter life becomes. You stop struggling to stay afloat and start gliding with the current.

To live in alignment, then, is to live awake, to participate in change without fear, to meet each moment as it comes, and to leave gracefully when it passes. In that awareness, the boundaries between you and existence dissolve. You are no longer a fragment trying to survive the flow; you are the flow itself, eternal, dynamic, and free.

PART II

UNDERSTANDING THE MIND AND ITS CREATIONS

5 POSITIVE AND NEGATIVE THOUGHT

Positive = Memory and Satisfaction-

Every positive thought begins as a reflection of something that has already been experienced, achieved, or understood. The mind draws upon memory, moments of success, affection, or joy, and recreates them in thought as evidence that life is good, that it is safe, that it is working in our favor. In that sense, all positive thoughts are past-oriented- they arise from memory and express satisfaction with what has already occurred.

When you feel confident, for example, it is not because confidence suddenly appears out of nowhere. It comes because your memory recalls a time when your actions succeeded, when effort brought reward. When you feel grateful, it is because your awareness visits moments that once nourished you. When you feel secure, it is because your mind remembers periods when things were stable. Even the optimism that points toward the future depends on the memory of past progress. It is the mind's way of saying, "Because I have succeeded before, I can succeed again."

Memory, therefore, is not only a record of the past; it is also a source of emotional stability. It allows the mind to find comfort in continuity. Positive emotions such as love, joy, and satisfaction are often grounded in the reassurance that something good has already existed. That remembrance gives life a sense of meaning and coherence. Without memory, every moment would feel new, but also uncertain, a continuous wave without the anchor of recognition.

Satisfaction, in turn, is the mind's way of acknowledging harmony between expectation and reality. It arises when what we hoped for and what we received come into alignment.

This alignment releases calm and pleasure in the body, neurochemical signals that tell the brain, "This is safe. This is good. You may rest now." Satisfaction completes a cycle that began with desire and effort. It provides closure, allowing the nervous system to relax, the heart to open, and the mind to become receptive again.

However, the peace created by satisfaction is delicate, because the mind quickly turns memory into attachment. It begins to chase the repetition of pleasant experiences, wanting them to return again and again. The positive thought, once gentle, becomes demanding- 'I must always feel this way." When that happens, memory stops being a source of contentment and becomes a source of longing. The same mechanism that gives joy starts planting the seeds of fear, the fear of losing what was once gained.

Understanding this balance is essential. Positive thoughts are not inherently higher or purer than negative ones; they simply arise from a different mental function. They are born from *recognition* rather than projection. The mind remembers, compares, and concludes, "I am happy," because it sees itself reflected in the memory of joy. Awareness, however, sees the movement behind both, the way the mind shifts from past to present, from memory to imagination, to sustain its sense of identity.

The spiritual purpose of positive thinking, then, is not to cling to pleasant memories but to use them as reminders that harmony is possible. A positive thought is a reflection of alignment, not its cause. The more we understand this, the less dependent we become on repeating external situations for internal peace. We begin to appreciate joy as a state of mind, not as a product of events.

True satisfaction arises not from recalling what has happened, but from recognizing that awareness itself, the one who remembers, is always whole. When we see that happiness is not in the memory but in the awareness of remembering, our relationship with thought changes. Memory still exists, but it no longer defines us. We become free to enjoy the sweetness of positive thoughts without the fear of their absence.

Negative = Projection and Uncertainty-

Every human mind is born with an instinct to protect itself. Deep within, it carries the memory of survival, an ancient intelligence that kept early life awake to danger. But in the modern world, where physical threats have largely been replaced by emotional ones, that same intelligence has not disappeared; it has evolved into something subtler, the projection of fear.

While positive thoughts arise from the comfort of memory, negative thoughts are born from the discomfort of imagination. The mind, unable to rest in uncertainty, begins to invent possibilities. It travels ahead of time, trying to predict what could go wrong. This is not an error in thinking; it is the brain's way of seeking safety in the unknown. The mind believes that by imagining the future, it can control it. In truth, it can only multiply it.

Negative thinking, at its core, is a form of mental insurance, a rehearsal for events that may never occur. It says,

"If I prepare for loss, I won't be shocked by it. If I expect rejection, I won't feel its sting. If I picture failure, I can learn how to avoid it."

On the surface, this seems logical, even mature. But beneath that logic lies the fear of uncertainty, the inability to live without knowing. The mind, in its craving for certainty, fills the blank space of the future with imagined scenarios, as though worry could substitute for wisdom.

This is how projection becomes the architecture of fear. Each "what if" thought is a brick in that structure-What if I fail? What if I lose what I have? What if I never recover? What if things don't improve? Every one of these questions tries to secure the future by predicting it. But the act of prediction itself fuels anxiety. The mind does not realize that its imagination, not reality, is the source of suffering.

When a person worries about a future conversation, failure, or event, the body reacts as though it were already happening. Heart rate increases, muscles contract, and the nervous system releases stress hormones. The physiological fear is real, even though the situation is not. This is how imagination, one of humanity's greatest gifts, becomes the architect of its own prison.

The irony is that the same imagination that creates fear also creates art, discovery, and love. The energy of imagination is neutral; its direction defines its outcome. When guided by curiosity, it leads to creativity. When guided by insecurity, it leads to anxiety. The mind uses the same tool to build beauty or to build fear, the difference lies only in awareness.

Projection also reveals a fundamental misunderstanding about control. The mind assumes that thinking about the future can change it, that worry is a form of preparation. But life unfolds through experience, not speculation. No amount of internal rehearsal can guarantee a specific outcome. The more we try to control what hasn't yet arrived, the more we disconnect from what *is* here. That disconnect breeds the very instability the mind hoped to avoid.

At the biological level, this behavior is rooted in ancient mechanisms. The amygdala, the brain's emotional alarm, cannot distinguish between imagination and perception. It reacts to thought as though it were fact. This is why imagining loss feels almost as painful as experiencing it. It's why fear can arise even in silence, in comfort, or in success. The body does not wait for reality; it obeys the mind's picture of reality.

Over time, this creates a feedback loop. The more one projects fear, the more evidence the mind finds to justify it. The imagination becomes the author of a self-fulfilling prophecy- "Because I feared it, I saw it; because I saw it, I feared it more." The mind becomes addicted to anticipation, mistaking anxiety for awareness. But true awareness is not tension; it is presence.

Presence dismantles projection. The moment one becomes conscious of this mental pattern, the endless forward rush of thought, the machinery slows. Awareness sees the mind manufacturing images of the future and recognizes them as imagination, not truth. The recognition itself dissolves the illusion. In that instant, the body relaxes, the breath deepens, and the nervous system receives a new signal- I am here, and here is safe.

To live without projecting fear does not mean to stop planning or preparing. It means to plan with clarity, not panic, to respond, not react. The wise mind still thinks about the future, but without confusing thought for fact. It recognizes that uncertainty is not a danger; it is possibility. Every invention, every love, every awakening has been born from uncertainty. Without it, life would have no space to grow.

Negative thoughts, therefore, are not enemies to be suppressed; they are signals to be understood. They indicate where trust has been replaced by control, where imagination has turned against itself. Awareness does not reject these thoughts; it listens to them gently. It asks, "What are you trying to protect me from?" In that compassionate inquiry, fear reveals its innocence. It is not here to harm, it is here to guard. And once awareness acknowledges it, it softens.

Eventually, one begins to see that uncertainty itself is sacred. It is not the absence of knowing; it is the birthplace of wisdom. It keeps life alive, flexible, open to surprise. When we stop projecting, we stop living in fragments of tomorrow and start living in the wholeness of now. The mind still imagines, but its imagination becomes creative rather than defensive. The same power that once built fear now builds freedom.

Why the Mind Over-Calculates the Future-

The human mind is a magnificent instrument, a living canvas that can imagine what does not yet exist. It can dream, design, and anticipate. This ability to project into the unseen has built civilizations, cured diseases, and mapped stars. Without imagination, there would be no progress. It is the divine spark that allows humans to participate in creation itself.

But what began as a gift for creation quietly became the seed of fear. The same imagination that paints visions of possibility also paints visions of disaster. The mind that can foresee beauty can just as vividly foresee loss. A single thought, What if this goes wrong?, can spiral into a storm of projections that feel as real as the present moment itself.

At its core, this is the paradox of the human brain: the power that allows us to invent also allows us to worry. When imagination loses balance, it turns from creativity into calculation, from vision into vigilance.

The Innocent Beginning-

The pattern begins innocently enough. The mind says, If I can predict the future, I can control it. If I can control it, I can stay safe. *It* believes that certainty will buy peace. So, it starts forecasting everything: outcomes, reactions, failures, conversations, even feelings.

Imagine someone preparing for a presentation. Instead of focusing on the material, their mind begins to loop: What if I forget a line? What if they don't like it? What if I embarrass myself? Within minutes, they've lived through a dozen imagined disasters that never happened. The body, unable to distinguish imagination from reality, responds with real adrenaline, real tension, real fear.

The same happens in daily life. A parent thinks of their child traveling alone, the mind instantly fills in worst-case scenarios. A worker receives a delayed email from a manager, the mind constructs possible reprimands. A person feeling slightly unwell imagines a diagnosis. The mind believes it is protecting, but in truth, it is producing suffering in advance.

The Habit of Over-Calculation-

Over-calculation is imagination caught in survival mode. It no longer creates; it defends. It constructs endless if–then chains, If I rest today, I might fall behind. If I speak honestly, I might lose approval. If I don't plan every detail, something will collapse.

At first glance, these thoughts seem responsible. Society often praises them as diligence or foresight. But the energy beneath them is fear disguised as reason. The more the mind calculates, the more it distances itself from the only real moment that exists, now. Life becomes an endless rehearsal, never a performance.

This happens because the mind mistakes life for a puzzle that must be solved perfectly. It assumes that with enough analysis, it can build a risk-free future, one without pain, loss, or uncertainty. Yet life is not a puzzle. It is a rhythm. It moves not in straight lines but in waves. When we try to control that movement, we lose harmony with it.

The irony is that the more we calculate, the less certain we feel. Every answer opens ten new questions. Every plan exposes ten new variables. And beneath the calculations, anxiety grows quietly, like roots beneath a polished floor.

The Memory Trap-

Much of this overthinking comes from memory. The mind remembers moments of pain and embarrassment, the job loss, the heartbreak, the criticism, and makes a secret vow: Never again. Then, every new situation becomes a test of that vow. The mind begins to live defensively, protecting against ghosts of the past.

For instance, a person who once lost money in business may analyze every future investment a thousand times. A person who once faced rejection may read hidden meanings into every silence. This is not prudence, it is trauma disguised as intelligence.

Over time, the mind starts treating all of life as a potential repetition of the past. It stops trusting the unknown and begins demanding guarantees. The present becomes conditional: I will live only when I am certain nothing will go wrong. But life never signs that agreement.

The Biology of Endless Prediction-

When imagination and fear merge, biology follows. The brain's threat centers, particularly the amygdala, cannot distinguish between real and imagined risk. When the mind envisions danger, the body releases the same stress hormones it would during an actual crisis.

Thus, even while sitting safely at home, the body may be living in survival mode. Heart rate increases, breath shortens, digestion slows, sleep lightens. Over time, this state of readiness becomes chronic. The system meant for quick reactions turns into a constant background alarm. The body feels like it's running a marathon that never ends.

This is why chronic overthinkers often experience physical exhaustion, muscle tension, shallow sleep, and poor concentration. The imagination, once a gift, begins consuming its own host.

Awareness: The Quiet Antidote-

The way out is not through control but through observation. When awareness watches the mind, really watches, without judgment or resistance, a small distance appears between the observer and the thought. In that space, breath returns, muscles soften, and perspective widens. You begin to see the stream of "what-ifs" as just that: thoughts, not prophecies.

Awareness doesn't stop planning; it purifies it. You can still think, still prepare, still build, but now you do it without panic. You plan not because you fear uncertainty, but because you love participation.

An aware mind says, Let me do my part sincerely, and let life handle the rest. It begins to trust that there is a larger intelligence at play, one that has guided stars, seasons, and oceans long before the human brain began predicting weather forecasts.

The wise do not abandon reason; they refine it. They think when needed and rest when not. They plan carefully but are never enslaved by plans. They understand that imagination is sacred when it serves creation, not when it feeds anxiety.

The Shift From Prediction to Participation-

When awareness matures, you stop trying to outsmart the future and start cooperating with it. You realize that life is not asking you to be omniscient, only to be present.

A painter does not predict each brushstroke before painting; they feel it. A musician does not foresee each note; they flow with rhythm. Likewise, a wise person does not try to control life; they dance with it.

You begin to see that the future is not an exam waiting to be graded. It is a conversation, between your awareness and the unfolding intelligence of existence. The more you trust that rhythm, the less you calculate.

Then, imagination returns to its rightful place, not as the engine of anxiety, but as the language of creation.

And in that shift, fear quietly transforms back into wonder.

6 THE CHAIN REACTION

Stress Between Effort and Expectation-

Stress is not the enemy of success; it is the friction between what we do and what we want to happen. It appears whenever effort collides with expectation, when reality moves slower, faster, or differently than the mind's design. In that gap, between what *is* and what should be, the tension of stress is born.

Every human being experiences this friction. It begins innocently, as motivation. You set a goal, imagine its reward, and start moving toward it. The effort feels exciting at first, charged with purpose. But as soon as progress wavers or outcomes delay, the mind begins to compare. It measures the distance between the ideal and the real. The greater the distance, the stronger the stress.

The Inner Friction-

Stress is not only psychological, it is physical. The body does not distinguish between the pressure of a deadline and the sight of danger. When expectations are unmet, the brain's alarm circuits activate the same survival system that once protected us from predators. Adrenaline rises, muscles tighten, and the heartbeat quickens. The body prepares to "fight or flee," though the threat now is invisible, an email, a task, a thought.

In this sense, stress is misplaced survival energy. It is the body's sincere but mistaken attempt to save you from disappointment. The more tightly you hold your expectations, the more the body fights for them. This constant fight drains vitality and clouds perception. You become reactive, restless, unable to feel satisfaction even in moments of rest.

The Illusion of Control-

At the root of stress lies an illusion, the belief that effort alone guarantees outcome. But effort operates within time; outcome belongs to life's rhythm. The mind confuses cause with control. It assumes that by working harder, thinking more, or pushing stronger, it can command the universe to follow its plan. When life refuses, stress blooms.

This is why high achievers often suffer most. Their vision is strong, but their attachment to that vision is stronger. They mistake persistence for resistance. Real effort is flexible; forced effort is rigid. The first flows with life, the second fights it. True success demands both drive and surrender, the ability to act fully, yet let go of the demand for certainty.

Expectations as Unconscious Contracts-

Every expectation is an unconscious contract with reality- "If I do this, life must give me that." When life does not sign the contract, we feel betrayed. But the betrayal is imaginary, reality never agreed to our terms. Stress emerges from this hidden misunderstanding.

The mind creates timelines and conditions, "by this age," "by this promotion," "by this result", and when they falter, identity trembles. We don't just lose control of the event; we lose the version of ourselves built around that event. Stress, therefore, is not only about work or outcomes, it is about identity trying to remain intact in a changing world.

Transforming Friction into Flow-

Awareness transforms stress not by removing pressure but by dissolving resistance. The moment you become conscious of the gap between effort and expectation, something shifts. You realize that the gap itself is not wrong, it is simply the space where learning happens. Every delayed outcome refines skill, patience, or perspective. The energy of stress, when observed without judgment, becomes focus.

This is not passive acceptance; it is intelligent cooperation. You still work, but you no longer argue with time. You still strive, but you no longer fear delay. When effort and awareness align, the mind's conflict softens. The same friction that once caused pain becomes the spark of creativity, the pulse of growth.

The Subtle Art of Surrender-

Surrender is not the opposite of effort; it is the completion of it. Once you have given your best, surrender allows energy to rest. It returns authority to life, to that vast intelligence that knows how to turn cause into consequence. In surrender, the body relaxes, the breath deepens, and stress dissolves. The nervous system finally receives permission to stop fighting what it cannot control.

The friction between effort and expectation will always exist; it is part of being human. But when met with awareness, it stops being suffering and becomes refinement. It polishes intention without burning the heart.

To live this way is to rediscover balance, to act fully, hope freely, and yet trust the rhythm that moves beyond your plan. Then, effort becomes expression, not exhaustion; and the absence of certainty no longer feels like danger, but like life breathing through you.

Anxiety as Imagination of Failure-

Anxiety is the mind's way of living in the future before the body has arrived there. It is not an emotion born from what *is* happening but from what *might* happen. While stress arises from friction between effort and expectation, anxiety begins where imagination turns that friction into a story of failure.

The anxious mind does not see events; it sees consequences. It runs ahead of time, projecting the worst possible outcomes and then reacts to its own predictions as though they were already real. In that sense, anxiety is not a reaction to life, it is a reaction to thought. The mind builds a world of possible disasters, and the body suffers as if it were living inside that world.

The Birthplace of Anxiety-

Anxiety begins the moment effort becomes evaluation. When the mind starts asking, "What if I don't succeed? What if this ends badly? What if I lose what I have?" the imagination takes control of reality. The event itself is neutral, a meeting, an exam, a decision, but the mind overlays it with scenes of rejection, embarrassment, or loss. It creates a movie of the future and forgets that it is the director, not the audience.

The tragedy is that these imagined failures rarely happen. Yet, the body cannot tell the difference between real and imagined threat. Every projection of failure triggers a real physical response, a racing heartbeat, shallow breath, tension in the stomach or chest. The nervous system enters defense mode without an enemy to fight. Over time, this false alarm becomes habitual, and anxiety becomes a lifestyle rather than a momentary state.

The Mind's Need for Certainty-

At the root of anxiety lies a deep human need- the need to know. The mind equates knowledge with safety. When it cannot predict an outcome, it fills the unknown with fear. It is not uncertainty itself that creates anxiety, but the mind's intolerance of uncertainty. It demands guarantees in a world designed to move.

The anxious mind seeks to secure the future by preparing for failure. It believes that constant worry will protect it, that by imagining pain now, it will suffer less later. But pain rehearsed is pain multiplied. Anxiety does not prevent failure; it prevents peace. It makes the present moment feel unsafe even when nothing is wrong.

When Imagination Becomes a Prison-

Imagination is the mind's most powerful tool. It can create art, solutions, empathy, and dreams. But when it is ruled by fear, it becomes a prison. The mind replays potential mistakes, magnifies small risks, and interprets every silence as a sign of danger. Even rest becomes uncomfortable because the anxious brain has forgotten how to stop scanning for threat.

This overuse of imagination narrows perception. A person lost in anxiety no longer sees what *is*, only what might be lost. Opportunities become risks; relationships become liabilities. The same creativity that could build a future becomes trapped in predicting its collapse.

The Feedback Loop of Fear-

Anxiety sustains itself through repetition. A fearful thought arises, the body reacts, and the reaction confirms the fear- "If my heart is racing, something must be wrong." This circular reasoning traps awareness in a self-feeding loop. The more the body reacts, the more real the fear feels. The more real it feels, the more the body reacts. The result is chronic tension, not caused by danger, but by imagination mistaken for danger.

Breaking this loop does not require fighting the mind but observing it. When awareness watches the mind spin its stories without joining them, the illusion loses power. You realize that the mind is merely doing its job, trying to keep you safe, but that its methods are outdated. In that moment, distance is created between you and the thought. The thought continues, but its grip loosens.

Awareness as Antidote-

The first step out of anxiety is recognition- seeing that fear of failure is imagined, not experienced. The body may still react, but awareness stays still. You begin to understand that anxiety is not a flaw in you, it is misplaced creativity. The same imagination that envisions failure can also envision success, understanding, or peace. The energy does not need to be suppressed; it needs to be redirected.

Mindfulness and breath become powerful tools here. Each deep, conscious breath reminds the body that it is safe. The mind, noticing the body's calm, slowly begins to follow. This simple communication, from awareness to physiology, rewires old patterns. Over time, the habit of imagining failure transforms into the ability to imagine possibility.

The Purpose Behind the Panic-

Seen deeply, anxiety is not punishment; it is a messenger. It shows you where your trust in life has fractured, where the mind is overstepping the heart. Every anxious thought says the same thing- "I do not trust what I cannot control." Awareness does not argue with that; it listens. It brings compassion to the frightened parts of the mind and shows them, gently, that life has never required certainty, only presence.

When awareness grows, imagination begins to serve consciousness rather than threaten it. The same mind that once created anxiety begins to create insight. The future, instead of being a field of danger, becomes a space of potential. Failure itself loses its sting, because you see that even if it arrives, it too will pass, just another change in the ongoing rhythm of life.

Anxiety ends not by controlling the future but by realizing that the future has never been the problem. It was always the imagination's projection of failure that made life feel unsafe. The moment you stop treating your thoughts as prophecies and start recognizing them as possibilities, the mind rests. And when the mind rests, life begins again, unburdened, alive, and open.

The chain of stress → anxiety → panic is not a curse, it is a signal. A signal that the mind has taken control of life's rhythm and the body is begging for release. Every link in this chain is created by the same invisible force- unconsciousness, the absence of awareness. And just as darkness disappears in the presence of light, this entire sequence dissolves when awareness awakens.

Awareness- The Inner Light-

Awareness is not another thought that the mind produces.
It is what sees thought.
It does not argue with the mind; it observes it.
It does not suppress emotion; it witnesses emotion.
And in that simple act of seeing, separation begins, you realize that you are not the storm, but the sky that contains it.

When awareness awakens, you stop drowning in your own experience. You begin to see thoughts, sensations, and reactions as movements occurring within you, not as you. The waves still rise, but you are no longer thrown by them. The seeing itself becomes the stillness.

In moments of stress, awareness functions like a mirror. It shows you the precise moment when effort turns into strain, when you cross from doing your best to forcing an outcome. It lets you notice how your body tightens, how your breath shortens, how your mind begins to measure your worth by results. And in that recognition, something remarkable happens: you pause. That pause is not weakness; it is wisdom. It interrupts the mechanical habit of reaction. You take a breath, and in that breath, the whole inner machinery resets.

In moments of anxiety, awareness becomes a lantern that exposes the imagination. It reveals how the mind quietly drifts into the future, scripting scenes of failure or rejection, mistaking thought for reality. You suddenly see that fear was never living in the future, it was living in your projection of it. The instant this is seen, imagination loses its authority. The story dissolves; only the watcher remains.

And in moments of panic, awareness becomes the anchor that holds you to the ground of being. You begin to realize that the body's reactions, the racing heart, the trembling hands, the rush of heat, are not betrayals but releases. They are waves of old fear finally leaving the system. Awareness helps you stay with these sensations without resistance, without labeling them as "bad." Each breath becomes a gentle permission: let it move, let it pass.

Over time, this witnessing changes the entire relationship with fear. You stop trying to fix your emotions and start allowing them to complete their natural rhythm. Stress becomes a signal instead of an enemy. Anxiety becomes imagination you can smile at. Panic becomes a clearing.

In this light of awareness, life no longer feels like a battle to win but a process to understand. You discover that peace was never the absence of disturbance, it was the presence of knowing.

The Science of Stillness-

For centuries, sages have spoken of awareness as the medicine for the restless mind. Today, science finally speaks the same language, in the quiet hum of brain scans and neural maps. Modern neuroscience reveals that when we watch our inner world without judgment, something extraordinary happens inside the physical brain.

In moments of mindful observation, when you notice your breath, your thoughts, or your sensations with patience instead of resistance, the brain's higher centers begin to awaken. The prefrontal cortex, the region responsible for reflection, empathy, and balanced decision-making, lights up. This area of the brain acts like an inner guide, translating raw experience into wisdom. It helps you see clearly rather than react impulsively.

At the same time, the amygdala, the brain's built-in alarm bell, begins to quiet down. The amygdala's job is to detect danger and trigger the body's fight-or-flight response. In a world filled with constant stimulation, this alarm is often left ringing. But under the light of awareness, it learns that not every thought is a threat, not every uncertainty is an emergency. Slowly, its signals soften. The body moves from alertness to calm, from defense to trust.

This shift is not imagination, it is measurable. As awareness deepens, the parasympathetic nervous system, responsible for rest, repair, and digestion, takes over. Heart rate slows. Breathing deepens. Muscles unclench. Blood pressure stabilizes. In this biological stillness, the body remembers its original rhythm, the same rhythm it knew in moments of safety, long before the mind began predicting danger.

Neuroscientists call this neuroplasticity, the brain's ability to change its structure and function through experience. Awareness becomes the sculptor. Every time you pause, observe, and return to the present, you are reshaping the neural pathways that govern stress and fear. Over time, the brain learns a new pattern: peace is safe. Calm is natural. Presence is strength.

This is not philosophy; it is physiology serving consciousness. What ancient teachers discovered through silence, modern science now confirms through evidence, that awareness is not passive; it is transformative.

Each moment of pure observation strengthens the circuitry of resilience and weakens the circuitry of reactivity. The brain begins to mirror the stillness of the observer itself. In other words, the more you rest in awareness, the more your biology learns to rest with you.

When this harmony is established, stillness is no longer an effort. It becomes your default state, not as withdrawal from life, but as clarity within it. The world continues to move, but your center no longer moves with it.

Awareness Is Not Control-

A common misunderstanding is to treat awareness as another tool of control- "If I stay aware, I will never feel bad again." But awareness is not manipulation, it's intimacy. It doesn't promise a life without pain; it promises a life without confusion. You will still face challenges, but they will no longer define you. You will still feel fear, but it will no longer enslave you.

Control tightens; awareness expands. Control tries to fix life; awareness learns from it. When awareness grows, life doesn't become perfect, it becomes real. And in reality, there is a quiet kind of freedom.

How the Chain Breaks

- Recognition, You begin to notice the pattern- stress starts with effort, turns into anxious imagination, and ends in panic. Naming it already breaks its momentum.
- Observation, You stay present with sensations, the racing heart, the shallow breath, without labeling them as "bad." You witness your body's protest without resistance.
- Reconnection, You bring the mind back to the body through breath. Breath acts as the bridge between thought and life.
- Release, In deep awareness, tension dissolves on its own. The nervous system finds rhythm again. You realize peace was never lost; only forgotten.

This is not an overnight practice. The mind has spent years building these habits; awareness gently unbuilds them, one moment at a time. But with each cycle observed, the chain weakens, until one day, it simply doesn't form anymore. Stress arises, you notice, and it melts. Anxiety knocks, and you smile. Panic whispers, and you breathe.

Living as Awareness-

Awareness is not something you "do"; it is something you remember. You are already the witness, the calm behind every storm, the silence between every heartbeat. Fear, stress, and panic are clouds that pass through your sky; awareness is the sky itself. Once you realize this, you stop trying to escape storms, you start trusting that none of them can break the sky.

Living this way transforms your very relationship with existence. Life stops being a problem to solve and becomes an experience to dance with. Work becomes play, rest becomes sacred, and challenges become invitations to grow. You are no longer surviving your thoughts, you are observing them, learning from them, and letting them flow.

This is how the chain breaks, not through willpower, but through wisdom. You stop being the prisoner of thought and become its observer. You stop resisting change and begin flowing with it. You stop fighting life and start living it.

And when that happens, something extraordinary unfolds, the same energy that once created fear becomes the energy that reveals freedom.

7 ROLE OF THOUGHTS

The Sacred Role of Thoughts in the Design of Life-

No one can look at this world closely and fail to notice its pattern of twos. Day and night, sky and earth, sound and silence, man and woman, birth and death, joy and sorrow, everything that exists seems to have its counterweight. The very rhythm of life depends on this pairing. If there were only day, how would the meaning of night be known? If there were only sound, how would silence soothe? The universe is a balance of opposites, and it sustains itself by their conversation.

It is difficult not to wonder- Why was it designed this way? Why couldn't everything be good, beautiful, peaceful, and bright? If an all-intelligent power shaped the cosmos, why not remove contrast entirely? The answer, though subtle, lies in the fact that contrast itself is the proof of consciousness. Awareness awakens only when there is something to compare. Without difference, there is no recognition; without recognition, there is no experience. Life would be blank, motionless, and meaningless.

The entire creation moves through this law of dual expression. Fire both warms and burns. Water both nourishes and erodes. Wind both refreshes and destroys. Each force carries two possibilities, and their balance gives the world its structure. It is not punishment or cruelty that both sides exist, it is necessity. Without opposition, there can be no motion, and without motion, nothing can evolve.

The same law that governs stars and oceans governs the human mind. The mind, too, was built with two forces that mirror the architecture of the universe, positive and negative thought. Both are essential for the simple reason that human beings are participants in this larger system, not spectators of it. The mind must reflect the design of the world it lives in.

Positive and negative thoughts are not accidents. They are deliberate elements of the mechanism that keeps life intelligent and adaptive.

Positive thought propels; negative thought protects. One invites expansion; the other demands reflection. One moves outward, seeking growth, connection, and creation; the other moves inward, seeking balance, caution, and self-correction. Together, they sustain the inner ecology of consciousness.

If there were only positive thoughts, human beings would live in constant excitement, blind to danger, deaf to discipline, incapable of empathy. A mind that knows only joy would never learn the meaning of humility. It would chase pleasure without pause and mistake ignorance for bliss. The presence of negative thought prevents that blindness. It reminds the mind that existence has depth. Fear instructs caution, doubt asks for clarity, and grief teaches appreciation. These so-called negative emotions are not intruders; they are teachers.

Think for a moment about the structure of the body. Every inhale must be followed by an exhale. Every heartbeat alternates between contraction and release. The very act of being alive depends on rhythm, the dance of opposite movements that create one continuous flow. In the same way, mental and emotional life requires alternation. The highs and lows of thought are not signs of instability; they are signs of vitality.

Negative thoughts do not arrive to punish you for imperfection. They arrive to signal imbalance, a reminder that something in your internal world needs understanding. When you feel fear, your system is asking for safety. When you feel anger, it is asking for boundaries. When you feel jealousy, it is asking for self-worth. Every unpleasant thought is carrying a message that, once decoded, helps restore equilibrium.

Positive thoughts, on the other hand, are not random gifts. They arise when alignment occurs, when your values, choices, and actions move in harmony. Gratitude, contentment, and inspiration are evidence of internal order. They appear when the energy of life flows unobstructed through mind and body. But they are not meant to stay forever, because stagnation even in joy leads to emptiness. The cycle must continue, reflection after expansion, stillness after motion, for awareness to deepen.

If we look closely, we will see that the purpose of both types of thought is not emotional pleasure but understanding.

Life is less concerned with keeping us comfortable than with keeping us conscious. A mind filled only with happiness would never grow beyond its comfort zone; a mind filled only with struggle would collapse from fatigue. The alternation between the two creates maturity, a steady intelligence that neither denies pain nor clings to joy.

The world outside mirrors this truth. The earth needs both rain and sun to flourish. Too much of either destroys the balance. The same holds within. Positive thoughts nourish; negative thoughts prune. Together they make the garden of the mind capable of renewal.

When you observe your thoughts in this way, something profound happens. The constant labeling of "good" and "bad" begins to lose meaning. You see that both have value, and both belong. This understanding dissolves unnecessary conflict with your own mind. Instead of fighting against thoughts, you begin to cooperate with them, using positive thoughts as direction and negative thoughts as information.

Over time, you realise that every human being, regardless of culture or belief, lives inside the same design. We all think, feel, desire, and fear because that is how the universe experiences itself through us. Thought is not a personal defect but a universal function. Even the most painful ideas are not foreign intrusions; they are part of life's dialogue with itself.

If you could step back far enough and look at existence as a single unfolding story, you would see that nothing in it is wasted. The laughter, the sorrow, the certainty, the confusion, all contribute to the same movement of learning. Positive and negative thoughts are the script through which consciousness expresses both its curiosity and its caution. They are how the infinite experiences the finite.

This is why, despite our resistance, the alternation between joy and pain persists. It is the mechanism by which human beings evolve from instinct to awareness, from reaction to understanding. The divine intelligence, whatever name one prefers to give it, wrote contrast into creation not as cruelty but as compassion. For only through contrast can awareness remember itself.

When this is seen, life stops feeling like a battlefield of emotions and starts to look like a conversation. Each thought, whether bright or dark, becomes part of a greater dialogue guiding you toward wholeness. The question shifts from "How can I get rid of this thought?" *to* "What is this thought trying to teach me?"

And that is where transformation begins. You are no longer ruled by polarity; you are educated by it. Positive and negative thoughts lose their opposition and reveal their shared purpose- to awaken intelligence, to refine perception, and to sustain balance in the vast system of living energy that we call existence.

How fear, pain, and doubt awaken empathy and faith

Fear - Awareness of Fragility-

Fear has always been one of life's most misunderstood emotions. From childhood we are told not to be afraid, as though fear itself were an enemy we must conquer or hide. Yet fear is not a flaw in the design of the human mind; it is an intelligent signal built into every living being. It exists not to paralyse us, but to protect us, to sharpen attention and remind us that life is precious and easily lost.

If we observe it closely, fear is not chaos, it is awareness in motion. The body tightens, breath quickens, the senses become alert. All these are signs of heightened attention. Something inside us whispers, "Be careful. Pay attention. Something important is at stake." Without this whisper, we would walk through fire without hesitation or stand at the edge of cliffs without respect for gravity. A world without fear would not be peaceful; it would be reckless. Fear gives life its depth and dimension of care.

When fear arises, it is usually pointing toward something valuable, someone we love, a goal we cherish, a part of identity we don't want to lose. In that sense, fear acts as a mirror reflecting what matters most. Instead of asking, "Why am I afraid?" it helps to ask, "What is so important to me that fear has come to protect it?" The answer to that question often reveals the heart of our priorities, the hidden layers of affection and meaning that guide our choices.

Consider the simple fear of losing a loved one. Beneath it lies love itself, the wish that the bond never ends. Or the fear of failure, beneath it lives the desire to create, to be capable, to do something meaningful. Fear appears as a shadow, but the source of that shadow is almost always light. When we follow it back to its origin, gratitude is waiting there.

Seen this way, fear becomes a teacher of appreciation. It reminds us that nothing we love is permanent and that life's fragility is what gives it beauty. The flower's charm lies in its brief bloom; the sky's grandeur moves us precisely because the sunset fades. If everything were certain and eternal, there would be no tenderness, only repetition. Fear's quiet wisdom is that love without awareness of loss is shallow; to love deeply, we must also acknowledge impermanence.

Many people try to fight fear by denying it, yet denial only drives it deeper into the body. Fear that is repressed turns into anxiety, a low hum of tension that never seems to stop. The way out is not suppression but attention. When fear is allowed to speak, it becomes understandable. If you sit with it, breathe, and listen, it begins to reveal its logic. You realise it was not here to harm you, it came to warn, to guide, to focus you on what needs care.

Every major act of courage in human history has included fear. Courage is not the absence of it; it is the decision to move through fear with awareness. A pilot flying through turbulence, a doctor performing emergency surgery, a parent standing firm for a child, all feel fear. Their mastery lies not in eradicating it but in cooperating with it. Fear provides the energy; awareness provides the direction. Together they create action that is both alert and compassionate.

Fear also cultivates humility. It reminds us that we do not control everything, that there are forces larger than our plans. When a storm arrives or an illness strikes, fear draws our attention to the delicate balance between human effort and the unpredictability of life. It teaches respect for limits and awakens a deeper trust in something beyond calculation.

In relationships, fear encourages empathy. When you know what it feels like to tremble, to worry, or to lose sleep over uncertainty, you recognise that same trembling in others. You no longer dismiss another person's fear as weakness; you recognise it as humanity. The simple sentence "I understand" often carries more comfort than any solution, and that understanding is born from your own moments of fear.

When approached with awareness, fear gradually transforms. It becomes gentler, less like an enemy and more like an inner guardian. It stops being a force that closes the heart and becomes one that opens it. You still feel its arrival, the quickening pulse, the tension, but instead of panicking, you pause. You acknowledge, "Yes, I'm afraid. That means I care. Let me act carefully, not carelessly."

With time, you begin to notice that fear is cyclical. It rises, teaches, and passes. Each cycle leaves you a little wiser, a little more capable of balance. You start trusting that even fear has purpose and that its energy can be redirected into clarity. The same fire that once burned can illuminate.

The next time fear appears, try meeting it with curiosity rather than resistance. Ask it what it wants you to see. Perhaps it will show you a part of life you have been taking for granted. Perhaps it will reveal a hidden strength or remind you to slow down. If you treat it as a messenger rather than a monster, it will start to speak in a softer voice.

Ultimately, fear keeps the living world attentive. It is the pulse that maintains vigilance, the reminder that life, though temporary, is worth every ounce of care. To live without fear would be to live without reverence. To live wisely with fear is to recognise fragility, cherish what you have, and act with mindfulness.

When that understanding dawns, fear no longer stands against you, it stands beside you, holding a lantern. It guides your steps through uncertainty, teaching you not only how to survive, but how to value everything that survival protects.

Pain- The Doorway to Empathy-

Pain is the most honest experience of being alive. It cannot be faked, avoided forever, or passed to another person. It arrives uninvited, stays as long as it must, and leaves quietly after teaching what words could never explain. Most of us meet pain as an enemy, something to endure or escape. But if we look closer, we begin to see that pain is not here to destroy us, it is here to make us feel, to awaken a depth that comfort alone could never reach.

When everything in life goes smoothly, awareness tends to shrink. We move from one task to another, counting days instead of living them. It is only when pain strikes, through loss, rejection, failure, or illness, that we pause long enough to ask what really matters. Pain has a way of stopping time.

It clears away distraction and brings attention back to the heart. In that stillness, something remarkable begins- we start to feel again, not just exist.

Pain humbles the human spirit. It shows us that no one is beyond vulnerability. The strongest mind, the wealthiest body, the most confident soul, all eventually meet moments they cannot control. This realisation softens judgment. You no longer see people as winners and losers, successful or failed. You see them as travellers, each carrying invisible weights, each trying to keep walking despite them. That understanding is empathy in its purest form.

Empathy doesn't come from books or theories. It grows from the soil of personal experience. When you have been lonely, you notice loneliness in another's eyes. When you have known loss, you handle another's grief more gently. When you have been misunderstood, you listen to others with patience. Pain dissolves the walls of separation that comfort quietly builds. It reminds us that beneath our differences, we all share the same nervous system of feeling, the same heart that can ache and heal.

There is a quiet dignity in people who have known pain and learned from it. They rarely speak loudly, but when they do, their words carry warmth. They have no interest in proving strength, because they have already faced weakness and survived it. Their kindness is not decoration, it's understanding in motion. You can sense in them the difference between sympathy and empathy- sympathy says, "I feel sorry for you," while empathy says, "I see myself in you." That bridge of shared humanity is built by pain.

Pain also shapes perspective. It rearranges priorities without asking permission. Things once considered urgent, a missed call, an argument, a delayed success, begin to lose their weight. You start valuing time, relationships, and peace in a way that only those who've lost them can. This quiet re-ordering of values is not failure; it is the soul maturing.

It is not necessary to seek pain to learn from it; life will deliver enough on its own. But it is necessary to meet it consciously when it arrives. Most suffering grows not from the pain itself, but from resistance to it. We tighten, protest, and replay the wound in our mind until it multiplies. Pain, when resisted, becomes chronic; when embraced, it becomes instructive. To sit with pain, to breathe through it without judgment, is to give it permission to speak its language.

That language, once understood, becomes wisdom. Pain teaches patience by refusing to leave quickly. It teaches gratitude by contrasting comfort. It teaches resilience by showing that healing is slow but certain. Every scar is a signature of survival. Every healed wound becomes a map of strength.

Over time, something subtle changes inside you. You stop fearing pain as a threat and start recognising it as a messenger. It becomes a signal of transformation. When a tree loses its leaves in winter, it looks barren, yet deep inside it is preparing for spring. In the same way, when pain empties you, it is making room for renewal. The hollow it creates becomes the space where empathy grows.

People often ask, "Why must growth hurt?" The answer is simple- because real growth changes structure. When you stretch a muscle, it resists before it strengthens. When you open the heart, it must crack the shell of old beliefs. Pain is that stretch, the body and mind adapting to new understanding. Without it, you might remain comfortable but small; with it, you evolve.

Pain also binds human beings together across distances and differences. It is the one experience everyone understands regardless of language, culture, or status. When you speak of loss, even strangers nod quietly. The details differ, but the feeling is universal. Pain strips away identity and reminds us that we are made of the same tenderness.

And yet, pain has one more gift often overlooked, it prepares the ground for joy. After enduring it, joy feels richer, more real. You no longer take happiness for granted; you savour it. You stop chasing constant pleasure and begin to appreciate simple peace. Pain deepens the capacity for gratitude because it reveals contrast. The warmth of sunlight is never so comforting as after a long cold night.

To walk through pain consciously is to graduate from avoidance to understanding. You learn that suffering is not the same as pain. Pain is the physical or emotional event; suffering is the story the mind tells about it. When the story softens, pain passes through you instead of taking residence. What remains afterward is clarity, an understanding of others, of life, of yourself.

The truth is, pain is not here to punish; it is here to connect. It opens doors that comfort keeps closed. It shows us that strength is not about never breaking but about continuing to love after breaking. When you finally see this, you stop asking, "When will the pain end?" and start asking, "What is it teaching me?"

In that moment, empathy awakens, not as a concept, but as a living force. You begin to see the world differently. Every person you meet becomes a reflection of your own journey, another being who feels, struggles, and hopes just as you do. You start walking more gently through life, aware that everyone is carrying something unseen.

And when you reach that level of seeing, pain has fulfilled its purpose. It no longer needs to stay. It has already transformed itself into compassion, the quiet power that binds humanity together.

Doubt, The Seed of Faith-

Among all emotions that shape human life, doubt is perhaps the most quietly powerful. It rarely enters like fear or pain, loud and demanding attention. It arrives softly, as a question- "Are you sure?" And in that moment, something begins to shift inside. Doubt can shake beliefs, unsettle routines, and make us question everything we thought we knew. Yet, this is exactly why it is sacred. Doubt is not the enemy of faith; it is the beginning of it.

For many, doubt feels like betrayal. It challenges what we have been taught to hold as certain. We equate doubt with failure, as if asking questions means we have lost trust in life. But the truth is far more generous. Doubt exists not to destroy belief, but to purify it. It is the natural mechanism by which the mind checks whether what it believes still matches what it knows through experience.

When you accept something blindly, your belief is fragile. It stands only as long as conditions support it. The moment life tests you, that surface confidence collapses. But when belief has been refined through doubt, it gains depth. It becomes more personal, more resilient, more real.

Imagine a tree growing in a greenhouse. It stands upright, shielded from wind and weather. It looks perfect, but its roots are shallow. Once planted outside, the first storm uproots it. Now imagine another tree, one that has grown in open ground. It has bent in the wind, lost branches, and faced drought. It may not look flawless, but its roots are deep, anchored in strength. That is the difference between faith that has never known doubt, and faith that has been shaped by it.

Doubt makes the mind alive. It keeps curiosity from dying into complacency. It makes us look again, question assumptions, and rediscover meaning. Without doubt, there would be no science, no philosophy, no art, no inner growth. Everything would stagnate in repetition. The human spirit evolves only when it dares to ask, "What if there is more?"

Doubt is also the birthplace of humility. When certainty breaks, ego softens. You realise that knowledge has limits, that life is larger than ideas. This recognition does not make you weaker, it makes you wiser. It opens a space where learning can happen. People who have doubted deeply often emerge more gentle, more understanding. They no longer need to convince others, because they have learned to live peacefully with not knowing everything.

But doubt can become dangerous when misunderstood. If we get trapped in endless questioning without reflection, the mind can spiral into confusion. Doubt, by nature, is movement, it must lead somewhere. It's like a wave- its purpose is not to stay suspended but to rise, break, and return to stillness. The goal of doubt is not permanent scepticism; it is clarity. The moment it fulfils its role, to push you toward understanding, it disappears naturally.

When handled consciously, doubt becomes a refining fire. It burns away imitation and illusion. It leaves behind only what your own experience can support. Through it, belief transforms into faith, not borrowed, not taught, but known from within.

Faith born from doubt is not naïve optimism. It is quiet assurance that life, even when uncertain, contains an underlying order. It is trust without proof, confidence without control. Such faith does not rely on everything going right; it rests on the understanding that even what goes wrong carries purpose.

When you stand in doubt, you are standing at the threshold of transformation. One side holds comfort; the other holds truth. To step through takes courage. But once you do, you begin to see that uncertainty is not emptiness, it is potential. Every genuine discovery, every creative act, every spiritual realisation begins with someone daring to doubt what was previously accepted as final.

Doubt also teaches patience. It does not offer quick answers. It slows the mind, forcing it to explore rather than assume. In a world obsessed with instant conclusions, doubt keeps the process of thought alive. It teaches us to sit in the unknown without panic, to breathe in questions without rushing to closure.

As the mind matures, doubt and faith stop appearing as opposites. They become partners. Doubt tests faith; faith stabilises doubt. Together, they form the foundation of genuine understanding. Faith without doubt turns rigid; doubt without faith turns hollow. But when they coexist, life gains both movement and meaning.

When you encounter doubt, try not to silence it. Welcome it as a teacher checking the roots of your conviction. Let it ask its questions. Let it shake what must be shaken. If your belief is true, it will stand stronger afterward. If it was false, you will be free. Either way, doubt has done its work.

What remains, after this refining process, is not the blind faith that avoids questions, but the luminous faith that includes them. A faith that says, “I do not know everything, but I trust the unfolding.” This is not the faith of certainty; it is the faith of understanding.

And that, perhaps, is life’s quiet secret- that doubt was never meant to end faith, but to complete it. It leads us from imitation to authenticity, from dependence to discovery, from assumption to awareness. When seen this way, doubt is not a storm that destroys belief, it is the rain that nourishes it.

The Sequence of Transformation-

When we look at life not as a series of random events but as an intelligent design of growth, a profound pattern emerges- fear, pain, and doubt are not separate intruders; they are interconnected stages of evolution. They appear one after another, guiding the human mind from unconsciousness to awakening. Each plays a sacred role, fear alerts, pain refines, and doubt awakens. Together, they sculpt awareness into wisdom.

Fear is always the first visitor. It knocks on the door of awareness to announce that change is near. It heightens sensitivity, pulls attention to what truly matters, and prepares the ground. Fear is the signal that the familiar is ending. Something old is dissolving, and something new is trying to take shape. In that brief gap, between what was and what will be, fear rises to remind us of our limits. It humbles the arrogance of certainty and opens a window for learning.

But fear alone cannot transform us. It can only alert us. When fear stays too long or remains unexamined, it becomes anxiety. That's when pain arrives, not as punishment, but as pressure that forces growth. Pain pushes us beyond avoidance. It makes us confront what fear only pointed to. Pain asks for action, for healing, for attention. It is fear translated into sensation, a message that something in the system, mind or body, needs balance.

Pain turns abstract fear into something personal, something you can feel, hold, and eventually understand. It takes you from "something might be wrong" *to* "something is wrong, and I can face it." And in facing it, you grow stronger, more compassionate, more human. Pain takes what was once a mental whisper and carves it into experience. It grounds learning in the body, in the heart. That's why lessons born from pain stay, they are written not in memory alone but in our very structure of being.

When pain reaches its peak and we've wrestled with it enough, doubt enters like a quiet observer. It doesn't hurt, but it unsettles. After pain has burned through illusion, doubt asks- "What now? What do you truly believe after all you've seen?" It's a question that refines consciousness. Fear wakes you up; pain humbles you; doubt redefines you. These three together form the alchemy of inner transformation.

If we resist this sequence, we suffer. But if we allow it, life begins to feel almost intelligent in its timing. Fear arises to make us alert. Pain follows to make us attentive. Doubt arrives to make us aware. And awareness is the seed of liberation.

Think about the times in life when you have changed most deeply. Perhaps it was after a loss, a heartbreak, or a challenge that seemed unbearable. First came fear- "I can't survive this." Then pain- "This hurts more than I thought." Then doubt- "Maybe there's another way to see this." What followed, slowly, was clarity, a new version of you, wiser, calmer, more compassionate. You didn't become this new version in spite of fear, pain, and doubt, you became it because of them.

In nature too, this pattern repeats. The seed must split before it sprouts; that moment is its pain. The sprout must push through dark soil, uncertain where the light is; that is its doubt. The entire process begins when the seed first senses the pressure of change, that is its fear. Without this friction, nothing new can be born. Every transformation, whether of a seed, a soul, or a civilization, requires this trinity.

Modern life, however, teaches us to avoid all three. We distract ourselves from fear with constant noise, numb pain with entertainment, and silence doubt with shallow certainty. We chase comfort as though comfort were the goal of existence. But comfort does not create consciousness, it only prolongs dormancy. Growth needs tension. Like a string on a violin, if it's too loose, it makes no sound; if it's too tight, it snaps. The art of living lies in finding that right tension, the place where awareness sings.

Fear, pain, and doubt are that sacred tension. They keep life awake, alive, and evolving. The person who avoids them stays the same; the one who understands them becomes wise. Wisdom is not freedom from fear, it's friendship with it. It's the ability to see pain not as cruelty but as correction, and doubt not as confusion but as cleansing.

The moment you accept this pattern, you begin to move through difficulty differently. When fear appears, you no longer panic; you listen. When pain arises, you no longer resist; you learn.

When doubt questions your certainty, you no longer defend; you explore. Life, instead of feeling like a series of battles, begins to feel like a classroom, a place of continuous refinement.

Every spiritual and psychological tradition, at its heart, points toward this same cycle. Not in religious language, but in the natural logic of consciousness. To awaken, one must first be shaken. Fear shakes. Pain breaks. Doubt remakes. Together, they clear the fog of assumptions and bring you back to direct experience, the only place truth can be known.

It is not an easy journey, but it is a sacred one. Because at the end of this process lies something subtle but profound- peace. Not the peace of escape, but the peace of understanding. You no longer need to control life, because you see that even its storms serve a purpose. You no longer crave guarantees, because uncertainty itself becomes the teacher. You stop asking "Why is this happening to me?" and start seeing "This is happening for me."

That shift, from resistance to participation, is the essence of awakening. And it begins not in joy, but in fear, pain, and doubt. They are the gates through which every soul must pass to discover its true strength.

When you look back one day, you may realize that your greatest growth did not come from what you avoided, but from what you endured with awareness. The nights you cried, the days you questioned, the fears you faced, those were not detours from your path; they were the path.

So, the next time fear knocks, pain stays, or doubt whispers, remember- they are not strangers. They are sacred messengers working together for your becoming. Welcome them. Listen to them. Learn their rhythm. Because once you understand how they dance together, you stop fearing the darkness and start trusting the design.

How joy and confidence bring creativity and celebration-

The Emergence of Joy-

When the storm within finally begins to settle, something subtle and astonishing happens. What remains is not silence alone, but a kind of light, calm, alive, and quietly radiant. This is joy. Not the loud happiness that depends on external victories, not the excitement that fades after a celebration, but the steady pulse of being itself, an ease that needs no reason to exist.

Joy is not a reward. It is not something that has to be achieved or maintained. It is the natural state that arises when fear, pain, and doubt have done their sacred work and released their grip. It appears when resistance disappears, the way sunlight fills a room the moment the curtains are drawn. Nothing new is added; only what blocked the light is removed.

For most of us, joy feels elusive because we are trained to chase it rather than to uncover it. We look for it in success, recognition, relationships, or possessions. We spend years building conditions around us, believing that joy will enter once everything is perfect. Yet every time we reach that imagined "perfect moment," joy slips away again. Why? Because joy cannot be possessed. It can only be allowed.

Joy is not the opposite of sorrow, it is the depth beneath both. When awareness deepens enough, joy and sorrow are seen as different notes in the same song of existence. The surface may change, one moment bright, the next quiet, but the music continues. The wise do not cling to the high notes or reject the low; they listen to the harmony. That harmony is joy.

The mind that has gone through fear learns attentiveness.
The heart that has gone through pain learns compassion.
The soul that has gone through doubt learns faith.

And together, they create the capacity for joy, because only a heart that has known depth can hold light without trembling.

Joy begins to arise when the struggle with "what is" ends. When we stop trying to fix, force, or fight life, the mind relaxes into acceptance, and acceptance opens the gate to peace. This peace, once recognised, begins to flow as joy. It is not excitement; it is restfulness with awareness. It is the simple contentment of being here, breathing, witnessing, without the constant need to become something else.

Children express this effortlessly. They laugh without reason, cry without shame, play without planning. Their joy is not a mood; it is their nature. The adult loses that not because life becomes harder, but because mind becomes noisier. Between expectation and regret, the space for joy shrinks. When we learn once again to live like a child, attentive but unburdened, joy returns, not as nostalgia, but as renewal.

The emergence of joy is also the proof that consciousness has matured. In early stages, awareness focuses on survival, protecting the body, acquiring resources, avoiding threats. Later, it moves toward expression, achieving, building, creating identity. But at a certain point, when the outer structures no longer define inner worth, awareness begins to turn inward. It asks, "Who am I beneath all this doing?" The moment that question ripens, joy begins to dawn, not from gain, but from understanding.

Joy is also the language of alignment. When your thoughts, actions, and inner truth move in the same direction, the energy they create is harmony, and harmony feels like joy. It is the feeling of being in rhythm with life, not struggling against it. Even when difficulties arise, something inside stays clear and unbroken. That is joy in its purest form, the still point within motion.

Many confuse joy with pleasure, but they are different in essence. Pleasure is born from contact, something touches your senses, and you feel momentary delight. Joy arises from connection, the invisible harmony between you and existence. Pleasure depends on external change; joy survives through every change. Pleasure ends when the experience ends; joy remains even when nothing happens.

A joyful mind is not naïve. It does not deny pain or pretend all is well. It simply understands that everything has its place. Joy is not the absence of darkness, but the presence of light that coexists with it. It is the understanding that sorrow, too, is sacred, that life, in all its contrasts, is a single unfolding experience.

In this sense, joy is the fragrance of wisdom. It comes only when you stop asking life to be otherwise. When you look at the same world you once feared, and now you see it not as a battlefield but as a garden, some flowers blooming, some fading, all part of one design, then you have begun to live in joy.

To live in joy does not mean constant laughter or unending peace. It means you no longer forget the sacredness of existence. Even when you cry, some quiet part of you still knows, "This too is life. This too is precious." That remembrance is joy.

The beauty of joy is that it expands naturally. It is contagious without effort. A joyful person does not need to preach or persuade, their presence uplifts. You feel lighter around them because their energy carries no demand, no heaviness of expectation. They have made peace with life, and that peace radiates silently.

Joy also awakens creativity. When the mind is no longer trapped in fear or comparison, it begins to play. Ideas flow freely; expression becomes natural. Joy does not ask, "Will this succeed?" It asks, "Can I share this?" That openness is what makes creation divine, not an act of ambition, but an act of participation in the universal flow.

The emergence of joy marks a turning point in every human journey. It is the dawn after a long night, not loud or dramatic, but gentle and certain. You begin to see that happiness was never missing; it was only covered by clouds of resistance. And just as the sky remains the same whether covered or clear, the essence of joy has always been within you, waiting to be noticed.

When you live in joy, you do not escape life, you enter it fully. You don't need everything to go right; you simply recognise that everything is part of the rightness of existence. You stop chasing meaning and start living meaningfully. And the miracle is that joy does not make you passive; it makes you alive. You begin to give without calculation, to love without defense, to act without fear.

That is the true emergence of joy, when being alive itself feels like a celebration.

The True Nature of Confidence-

Confidence has been one of the most misunderstood words in modern times. We are taught to equate it with boldness, with speaking louder than others, with the assurance that we are right. We celebrate the confident as those who never hesitate, never falter, never doubt. Yet true confidence has nothing to do with volume or dominance; it is not about standing above others, but about standing within oneself, quietly, fully, and with grace.

The confidence that most people chase is fragile. It depends on conditions, on approval, achievement, validation, and success. When those outer supports crumble, it vanishes. That is not confidence; it is attachment disguised as strength. Real confidence begins only when dependence ends. It arises not from what you possess, but from what you understand.

Confidence, in its purest essence, is trust, as trust in life, trust in timing, trust in one's ability to respond to whatever arises. It does not demand certainty, because it understands that certainty is an illusion. Life changes, people change, and outcomes are never guaranteed. Yet, amid all this uncertainty, confidence whispers- "I can meet whatever comes." It is not arrogance; it is alignment.

A truly confident mind does not need to prove anything. It is at peace with its strengths and honest about its weaknesses. It does not pretend to know everything; it simply knows that it will learn when needed. This kind of confidence does not shout, it shines. It moves with calmness, not aggression, because it knows that real power is quiet.

In the human journey, confidence emerges naturally after fear and doubt have been understood. When fear teaches you awareness and doubt teaches you humility, confidence arises as the balance between them. It is the middle ground between recklessness and hesitation. Like a perfectly tuned instrument, it neither strains nor slackens. It simply plays in harmony with the rhythm of life.

Confidence is not an external posture but an internal alignment. It appears when your thoughts, emotions, and actions point in the same direction. When you stop fighting yourself, when the mind no longer argues with the heart, confidence blooms effortlessly. It is the ease of coherence.

Most people spend their lives trying to build confidence, reading books, repeating affirmations, copying behaviors, without realising that confidence is not something to be built; it is something to be uncovered. It is always there, beneath layers of doubt and comparison. It is not added from outside but revealed from within when self-judgment dissolves.

The source of real confidence is self-understanding, not self-image. Image changes with perception; understanding stays. When you know your intent is pure, your actions are honest, and your efforts sincere, you no longer need constant reassurance. You move through life not as a performer, but as a participant. That is confidence.

Confidence also grows from integrity. When your inner truth matches your outer behavior, you stop fearing exposure. You do not need to maintain appearances or prove worth. Integrity makes you transparent to yourself, there is nothing hidden to protect, nothing false to maintain. From that transparency, confidence flows like clear water, calm, deep, and nourishing.

There is a grace in people who carry this kind of quiet assurance. They do not rush to fill silence or compete for attention. They listen with presence, speak with clarity, and act with intention. Their confidence is not a performance; it is an atmosphere. You feel safer around them because their energy is grounded. They don't drain others; they stabilize them.

Confidence, when misunderstood, often mutates into arrogance, a brittle mask covering insecurity. Arrogance is rooted in fear of inadequacy; it must constantly prove superiority. True confidence, however, is humble. It knows that strength without kindness is brittle, and humility without strength is incomplete. The mature mind holds both.

There is also a subtle beauty in how confidence interacts with failure. The confident person does not escape failure, they engage with it differently. They do not see it as personal loss, but as feedback from reality. Each fall becomes a correction, not a condemnation. Failure loses its sting because identity is no longer tied to outcome. Confidence, in this sense, is resilience wearing a smile.

At a deeper level, confidence is born from connection, the recognition that life itself supports you. When you stop seeing existence as a battlefield and start seeing it as a partnership, confidence arises effortlessly. You begin to feel that you are not a separate fragment fighting against the world, but a conscious part of its unfolding. This shift from "I must control" to "I can trust" transforms fear into faith.

Confidence also carries a quiet generosity. Because it is not rooted in insecurity, it celebrates others instead of competing with them. A confident person can admire without envy, guide without superiority, and learn without shame. They understand that everyone walks their own rhythm of becoming, and there is space for all.

Perhaps the simplest way to understand confidence is this- it is the natural posture of the soul when it is not bent by fear. When the weight of self-doubt lifts, you stand naturally tall, not on your toes, not on others, just on truth. You become steady not because life is predictable, but because your heart has stopped wavering.

Confidence does not promise that things will go well. It promises that *you will remain well* regardless of what happens. It is not the certainty of success; it is the certainty of self. When that understanding settles, a person can walk through uncertainty with the same ease as through clarity, because they no longer depend on conditions for peace.

In its highest form, confidence is an act of surrender. It says, "I trust this life enough to participate in it fully." It no longer resists experience, nor hides behind perfection. It moves through both ease and difficulty with the same composure, like a river that flows around rocks without losing its direction.

And this, perhaps, is the true secret- the more you trust the flow of life, the more confident you become in yourself, because you and life are not separate. Confidence, then, is not the armor of the ego; it is the nakedness of truth. It is standing in the middle of uncertainty with an open heart and steady breath, knowing that whatever happens, you will meet it with awareness.

Joy as the Fertile Ground of Creativity-

Every act of creation, whether it is painting a canvas, composing music, writing a sentence, designing a home, or nurturing a child, begins from the same invisible source, a moment of still, joyful openness. Creativity is not the privilege of artists or inventors; it is the most natural expression of an unburdened mind. When joy returns, creativity follows like fragrance after rain.

Creativity does not bloom in tension. It needs space, space inside the mind where ideas can breathe. A fearful, anxious, or constantly comparing mind is too crowded for imagination to land. The roots of creativity lie not in effort, but in freedom. That freedom comes when the mind is no longer trapped in judgment or expectation, when it is no longer obsessed with the outcome. In that moment, something larger begins to move through you, an effortless flow of inspiration.

When the mind is joyful, it becomes like a clear sky. Thoughts drift easily, patterns form naturally, and new connections emerge. You stop *trying* to be creative and begin allowing creation to happen through you. True creativity feels less like doing and more like witnessing. Something within you opens, something larger enters, and something beautiful takes shape between the two.

Joy and creativity are inseparable because both arise from the same state, presence. When you are present, you are not chasing results or replaying the past; you are alive in the current moment, completely absorbed in what is unfolding. This deep attention is the birthplace of all art, all innovation, all authentic expression. A joyful mind is not scattered; it is fully awake.

Most people confuse creativity with talent. They think only a few gifted ones can create something meaningful. But creativity is not a special skill; it is the natural state of consciousness when it is not trapped in fear. Every human being is born creative. We are all designed to shape life in our own way, to cook, speak, think, love, and build uniquely. What blocks creativity is not lack of ability but the habit of self-judgment. Joy dissolves that habit.

When you are joyful, you stop measuring yourself. You no longer compare your expression with others'. You don't write to impress, paint to please, or speak to be approved. You simply create because creation feels right. Joy makes you forget yourself, and in that forgetting, the truest part of you begins to express.

All great works, whether of art, discovery, or compassion, were born not out of pressure but out of play. Play is not childish; it is sacred. It is the spirit of creation itself. When you are playful, you are fearless; you are curious without agenda. You are open to surprise, willing to fail, and eager to try again. Play is joy in motion, and creation is its echo.

Creativity that springs from joy also carries healing. When you create from a joyful state, you are not just producing; you are aligning. The act itself becomes meditative, time disappears, effort disappears, even "you" disappear. What remains is flow, the same flow that moves rivers, grows trees, and forms galaxies. You are no longer separate from existence; you are participating in its dance.

This is why joyful creativity never exhausts you. It replenishes you. You can work for hours and feel refreshed, not drained. The body may tire, but the spirit glows. Because the energy behind your work is not tension but harmony.

When you observe deeply, you realise that creativity is not about adding something new to the world, it is about revealing what already exists in potential. Joy acts as the sunlight that awakens that potential. A joyful mind sees possibilities where a fearful one sees obstacles. It perceives patterns, connections, and meanings that anxiety hides.

Even in practical life, joy enhances intelligence. A joyful mind solves problems more easily, communicates more clearly, and collaborates more harmoniously. It is flexible and adaptive. It does not cling to one method; it experiments with delight. That is why creativity is not confined to art, it is needed equally in relationships, education, business, and daily living.

There is a deep connection between gratitude and creativity as well. When you are grateful, you recognise the abundance already present in your life. That recognition shifts your energy from wanting to giving. Creativity begins at that moment of inner abundance, when you feel full enough to share. A grateful mind expresses; a fearful mind accumulates. Joy and gratitude together make creation generous.

Some people fear that living in joy may make them passive, that they might lose ambition or drive. The opposite is true. Joyful people are often the most productive, not because they chase success, but because they love participation. They work with devotion, not compulsion. They are not motivated by lack, but by inspiration. Their work becomes a celebration of existence, not an escape from it.

Joy transforms creativity into service. You no longer create to be seen; you create to share. You no longer demand appreciation; you find fulfillment in the act itself. This is why the greatest creators, poets, scientists, philosophers, often describe their work as grace. They feel guided, as if something higher flows through them. That "something higher" is not outside, it is the intelligence of joy within them, freed from fear.

In its deepest form, creativity born from joy becomes prayer. Each stroke, each word, each note, becomes a way of saying, "Thank you for this life." And that is why true artists, inventors, and thinkers never really retire, because joy never retires. As long as awareness breathes, creation continues.

When joy becomes your ground, every act becomes creative. Cooking becomes art, conversation becomes poetry, work becomes meditation. You stop dividing life into "routine" and "special," because everything begins to feel alive. That is the hallmark of true creativity, when even the ordinary glows with presence.

And perhaps that is what life has been asking of us all along, not to achieve something extraordinary, but to live ordinarily with extraordinary awareness. Joy gives us that ability. It makes every moment fertile. Every breath becomes a brushstroke on the canvas of existence.

So if you ever feel uninspired or creatively blocked, don't chase new ideas, return to joy. Do something that makes you light again. Watch the sky, sit in silence, laugh with a child, listen to music, breathe deeply. When joy returns, ideas will too, effortlessly, playfully, beautifully.

Because joy is not just the background of creativity, it *is* creativity. It is life expressing itself through you. And when you allow that, creation ceases to be an act of doing; it becomes a state of being.

Confidence as the Force of Manifestation-

Every vision, no matter how luminous, remains only a shadow until it finds the courage to take form. Inspiration is the seed, but confidence is the soil in which it grows. Without confidence, creativity remains a dream, alive in thought but absent in the world. Confidence is the bridge between imagination and manifestation, between what is felt within and what becomes visible outside.

When joy opens the doors of creativity, confidence walks through them carrying purpose. It is the force that gives structure to inspiration, the quiet assurance that says, "This can be done." While joy creates possibilities, confidence chooses direction. One is the wind that lifts the sail; the other is the hand that steers the course.

Confidence in its truest form is not loud determination; it is gentle certainty. It does not rush to prove itself, it flows from alignment. You feel it not as tension but as steadiness, not as pride but as peace. It is not a declaration of superiority but an inner whisper of readiness. When you are in tune with your intention, confidence arises naturally, without being forced.

To manifest anything meaningful, this kind of confidence is essential. The world responds not to doubt, but to decisiveness. Life mirrors the state of your belief. When you move with clarity and quiet conviction, doors seem to open in synchrony. It is not magic, it is resonance. The universe echoes the energy you hold.

Confidence is also discipline in disguise. It does not merely say, "I believe." It acts, step by step, even when results are uncertain. It replaces perfectionism with progress. Each small action becomes a statement of faith, a way of saying to life, "I am participating." That participation is what transforms potential into presence.

But there is a fine balance here. Confidence and humility must walk hand in hand. Overconfidence blinds; under confidence paralyzes. True confidence stands between the two, firm yet flexible, certain yet open. It moves without arrogance, adapts without fear. Like a tree that bends in the wind but never breaks, such confidence knows both strength and grace.

When confidence is grounded in awareness, it becomes an energy of manifestation, not manipulation. You no longer impose your will on the world; you collaborate with it. The universe is not a field to be conquered but a partner to be harmonized with. You set an intention, you act with sincerity, and then you trust the process. That trust itself is confidence.

Confidence also protects creativity from self-doubt. Every creator, at some point, meets the inner voice that whispers, "Who are you to do this?" The joyful mind responds, "I am not special, I am available." That availability is confidence. It is not about believing you are greater than others; it is about realizing that you are capable of being a vessel for something greater than yourself.

Confidence transforms energy from hesitation into motion. Without it, ideas remain locked in hesitation; with it, even imperfect steps become progress. It is not that confident people never feel doubt, they simply do not stop there. They acknowledge doubt as a visitor, not a master. They move despite it.

At its core, confidence is the courage to begin. Every great journey, invention, and creation started with someone who dared to start before feeling ready. Confidence does not wait for the perfect moment; it makes the moment perfect through action. It turns thought into form, possibility into presence.

There is a beauty in how confidence interacts with failure. The insecure mind sees failure as proof of inadequacy; the confident mind sees it as feedback. Confidence doesn't avoid falling, it learns to fall gracefully. Every setback becomes a lesson in precision, every obstacle a teacher in patience. The truly confident are those who keep showing up, refining, adjusting, learning, and trusting.

Confidence also carries responsibility. Power without awareness becomes control; awareness without power becomes passivity. Confidence joins them, it empowers awareness to act and awareness guides confidence to act wisely. This integration makes human effort creative rather than destructive.

On a deeper level, confidence is spiritual participation. It is saying yes to existence. Every time you act with pure intention, you affirm the intelligence that created you. You align your will with the will of creation. This alignment makes manifestation effortless, not because challenges disappear, but because resistance within dissolves. You stop working against life and start working with it.

Confidence rooted in joy becomes service. It is not about proving worth, but expressing truth. Such confidence no longer asks, "Will this be appreciated?" It asks, "Is this true to my heart?" Once that answer is yes, the work proceeds with grace. Every effort becomes a prayer, every creation a form of gratitude.

Confidence also invites others to rise. When you stand steady in your authenticity, you unconsciously give permission for others to do the same. Confidence radiates safety; it inspires rather than intimidates. A confident person doesn't demand followers, they create more leaders. Their calm assurance reminds everyone around them that they, too, can trust their own light.

In daily life, confidence manifests in small gestures more than grand actions. It is in how you greet the morning, with openness instead of worry. How you listen to others, with presence instead of distraction. How you move through uncertainty, with curiosity instead of fear. Every such act says to life, "I am here, and I am willing."

Confidence, in its highest form, dissolves into surrender. It is no longer "I can do it" but "It can happen through me." This is not passivity, it is participation without ego. You no longer carry the weight of needing to control every detail; you allow life to co-create with you. The river does not force its flow; it simply moves with the terrain. That effortless movement is the essence of confident living.

When you begin to live from this place, manifestation becomes natural. You stop worrying about outcomes because you see that life itself is self-correcting. What is right for you finds you when you walk with integrity and openness. Confidence makes you patient enough to wait and wise enough to act when the moment comes.

And perhaps that is the quiet miracle of confidence, it transforms existence from a struggle into a dialogue. You no longer push against life; you converse with it. You no longer demand guarantees; you trust the rhythm. And in that trust, everything you are meant to create finds its way into being.

Celebration as the Natural End of Awareness-

When awareness matures, it does not end in silence; it ends in song. The mind that once trembled with fear, the heart that endured pain, and the spirit that walked through doubt finally arrive at a state so simple, so luminous, that the only response left is celebration. Not the loud, fleeting kind that depends on achievements or occasions, but the quiet celebration of being.

To celebrate life is to finally stop demanding that it be different. It is the full acceptance of "what is." It is the recognition that even imperfection carries its own strange perfection. Celebration arises when resistance dissolves, when you realise that life was never meant to be controlled, only to be experienced.

True celebration is not an escape from reality; it is intimacy with it. It does not deny pain or darkness; it includes them. It is the understanding that joy and sorrow, gain and loss, success and failure are not opposites but necessary movements of the same dance. Celebration is the moment when you stop asking, "Why is this happening to me?" and begin to whisper, "Thank you for allowing me to live this."

Celebration is awareness made alive. When the mind no longer divides experiences into good and bad, pleasant and unpleasant, it begins to see the underlying rhythm connecting them all. Everything becomes meaningful, the morning sunlight, the quiet evening rain, the laughter of a friend, even a solitary tear. Each becomes a verse in the poetry of existence.

A person who has learned to celebrate life is never poor. Their wealth is not measured in possessions but in perception. They carry an invisible abundance, the ability to find beauty where others see routine, gratitude where others see complaint. To them, each moment feels sacred, each breath feels like grace.

Celebration is also the highest form of intelligence. It shows that the mind has understood the futility of control and the beauty of surrender. A mind that celebrates no longer seeks constant improvement; it enjoys participation. Life stops being a race and becomes a dance. The dancer and the dance are no longer separate, awareness moves effortlessly through each step.

The mature mind doesn't celebrate only when things go right; it celebrates the very act of being alive. Even challenges become music to grow by. When pain arrives, you don't resist; you feel it fully, knowing it will refine you. When joy comes, you don't cling; you experience it deeply, knowing it will pass. This rhythm, of acceptance, experience, release, is the heartbeat of a truly awakened life.

Celebration does not mean a constant smile or a denial of difficulty. It is the capacity to stay open, even in hardship. It is the ability to see the hidden order behind apparent chaos. It is the understanding that even endings are beginnings in disguise. When you live with this awareness, every ordinary act becomes extraordinary, sipping tea, walking in silence, watching the sky change color. You no longer need grand reasons to feel alive.

Gratitude and celebration are two sides of the same coin. Gratitude is the inner acknowledgment of beauty; celebration is its expression. Gratitude feels; celebration shares. Gratitude is silent; celebration sings. When gratitude fills the heart, celebration naturally flows through action, art, and presence.

The most beautiful thing about celebration is that it dissolves separation. When you celebrate life, you stop seeing yourself as apart from it. You no longer stand outside, judging what happens; you are part of the happening itself. The wind that blows becomes your breath, the laughter of others becomes your joy, and the pain of another becomes your compassion. You begin to live not as an individual isolated in thought, but as consciousness flowing through all.

In this sense, celebration is prayer without words. You are not asking for anything, not complaining, not bargaining. You are simply saying yes, to existence, to change, to mystery. It is a state of gratitude so complete that it turns stillness into dance.

When awareness reaches this level, even the smallest act becomes sacred. You might be washing dishes, writing an email, or watering a plant, but something in you feels reverence. You are not doing for a result; you are doing for the joy of doing. That is the essence of celebration, action without anxiety, experience without expectation.

This is also where creation finds its highest purpose. When you create from celebration, you are no longer producing art or outcomes; you are expressing the overflowing fullness of being alive. The world does not need more perfect things, it needs more alive people. A person who lives in celebration contributes more light than a thousand well-intentioned plans.

Celebration also heals relationships. When you live with a celebratory heart, you stop expecting others to complete you. You meet them as equals in the joy of being. Conversations lose the weight of judgment. Love loses the anxiety of possession. Friendship becomes an exchange of laughter, not obligation. The other is no longer a mirror of your insecurity but a reflection of shared life.

As this understanding deepens, celebration becomes your default response to existence. You celebrate simply because you *are*. There is no reason needed. This kind of celebration doesn't need music, festivals, or applause; it happens quietly, in how you breathe, how you smile at a stranger, how you notice sunlight on the wall.

At the height of awareness, even silence celebrates. There is no noise, no dance, no words, only stillness pulsing with life. You begin to feel that existence itself is in a continuous celebration- the stars moving, the oceans breathing, the seasons changing. You are part of that rhythm, not separate from it. Life is not happening to you, it is happening through you.

When the seeker realises this, the search ends. There is nothing left to attain, nothing to escape, nothing to fix. There is only the joy of being aware, and in that awareness, celebration becomes the natural fragrance of the soul.

The Fine Line Between Creation and Collapse-

Every movement of life carries within it the seed of its opposite. Growth and decay, expansion and contraction, creation and destruction, they are not enemies, but phases of the same rhythm. The moment something begins to rise, the possibility of its fall is born alongside it. This is not a flaw in existence; it is its balance. It is the law that keeps the universe from tipping into chaos or stagnation.

The same is true within the human mind. Every great creation, whether a thought, a work, or a dream, stands on a razor's edge. Too little confidence, and the creation never takes shape; too much, and it collapses under its own weight.

Too little passion, and the spark fades before it catches fire; too much, and the fire consumes rather than illuminates. The difference between creation and collapse is not a difference of intent, it is a difference of awareness.

When the mind creates with awareness, it remains connected to the rhythm of life. It acts, expresses, and participates without attachment to outcome. Its energy flows in balance. But when awareness slips, even the purest creative impulse can turn into obsession. What began as inspiration becomes ambition; what started as joy becomes control. And what was meant to serve becomes something that enslaves.

Every human being has felt this shift. You begin a project with enthusiasm, a relationship with warmth, a goal with purpose, and somewhere along the way, the joy that began it turns into pressure. The mind tightens its grip; creation becomes compulsion. What was once an act of love starts feeling like a burden. You no longer flow with life; you push against it. That is the moment when creation begins to bend toward collapse.

Collapse does not happen because of failure. It happens because the mind forgets humility. When you start believing that you are the creator rather than the channel, the energy that once moved through you now begins to move against you. You start owning the creation instead of serving it. Pride replaces gratitude, and comparison replaces curiosity. The natural rhythm of giving and receiving breaks. The river of creativity, once fluid, begins to stagnate in the pools of ego.

Awareness keeps this balance intact. It reminds you that every act of creation, whether an idea, a business, a painting, or a relationship, is an exchange with life, not a conquest of it. You give form to something invisible, but the intelligence behind it remains larger than you. The moment you forget this, tension replaces grace, and effort replaces flow.

Creation without awareness breeds exhaustion. You can see it everywhere, people achieving great heights yet feeling hollow, building beautiful things but losing peace, collecting admiration but missing connection. Outwardly, they are creating; inwardly, they are collapsing. The foundation of creation is not success; it is stability of consciousness. When the inner base weakens, even the tallest structure begins to tremble.

Collapse also teaches. It reveals the parts of us that grew too fast, too rigid, or too proud. It returns us to humility, to stillness, to listening. Every fall is an invitation to rebuild differently, not from fear, but from understanding. It reminds us that the goal of creation was never permanence; it was participation. The universe itself is a rhythm of creation and dissolution, stars form and fade, cells divide and die, civilizations rise and evolve. To resist this rhythm is to resist life itself.

At the subtle level, creation and collapse share the same energy. The same intensity that drives a mind to create art can, without balance, drive it into chaos. The same sensitivity that makes someone deeply inspired can also make them deeply vulnerable. The line between genius and despair, passion and burnout, creation and destruction, is often invisible. Awareness is the light that makes that line visible.

Awareness means remembering the why behind the what. It means pausing in the midst of doing to reconnect with being. It means creating without losing yourself in creation. The more conscious you are of this balance, the more sustainable your expression becomes. You stop trying to hold on to every success, and you stop fearing every failure. Both are seen as waves in the same ocean.

When creation flows from ego, it seeks applause; when it flows from awareness, it seeks harmony. The first exhausts, the second replenishes. Awareness transforms ambition into contribution. It replaces the anxiety of outcome with the joy of participation. In that state, creation no longer collapses because it never tries to stand alone, it stands as part of the larger whole.

Collapse is not the end of creation; it is part of its renewal. Every structure must sometimes break to reveal a new form. Every identity must loosen for consciousness to expand. The universe itself breathes through this cycle of building and dissolving. When you see this clearly, even collapse becomes sacred, it is simply creation changing its direction.

To live in this awareness is to live wisely. You act fully but lightly. You create wholeheartedly but without possession. You celebrate the rise without fearing the fall. Because deep down you know that both belong to the same divine design. What begins must end, and what ends gives way to beginning again.

So walk that fine line consciously. Create with devotion, not domination. Let your hands shape the world, but let your heart remain humble. Remember that even the greatest creators are students of a larger intelligence. Stay open to correction, grateful for collapse, and aware that every ending is simply life adjusting its rhythm.

And when you can do that, when you can create and surrender, build and release, rise and bow, you will know the secret that has guided all of nature since the beginning - Creation and collapse are not opposites; they are breaths of the same eternal pulse.

Using Thoughts as Instruments of Awakening-

If you could look closely at the inner workings of the mind, you would see that thoughts are not enemies to be conquered; they are messengers. They come not to chain you but to awaken you. Every thought, pleasant or painful, noble or fearful, is part of a larger conversation that existence is having with you. Most people never listen deeply enough to understand what is being said. They either chase their thoughts or run from them, not realizing that both chasing and running keep them bound. The real art lies in learning to *listen.*

Thoughts are energy in motion, vibrations of consciousness expressing themselves in form. They arise like ripples on the surface of a lake. You cannot stop the ripples, but you can make the lake still enough that each ripple becomes clear. That stillness is awareness. When awareness watches a thought without judging, the thought loses its power to disturb. It becomes what it always was- information.

Every thought carries information about the state of your being. Fearful thoughts tell you where you feel unsafe. Angry thoughts reveal where you feel unheard. Loving thoughts show you where you are in harmony. Instead of labeling them good or bad, you can begin to see them as indicators, like signals on a dashboard. The purpose is not to destroy the signal, but to understand what it is pointing to.

When you begin to relate to thoughts in this way, a transformation occurs. The mind stops feeling like an adversary and becomes a mirror. You start noticing patterns- certain thoughts return again and again, as if asking for your attention. They are not curses; they are invitations. Every recurring thought is the psyche's way of saying, "Look here. Something needs understanding."

Awakening begins not by silencing thoughts, but by understanding their origin and movement. Just as a musician must first learn the notes before creating silence between them, the seeker must first learn the texture of thought before transcending it. Each thought has a rhythm, a pulse, a color. When you watch them without resistance, they start revealing the deeper architecture of your mind, the hidden fears, unhealed wounds, and forgotten wisdom that shape perception.

At this point, awareness begins to separate from content. You realize that you are not the thought itself, you are the space in which it appears. This realization is the turning point of all inner growth. Until then, you live as a prisoner of the mind's constant chatter, believing every word it says. But once you see that you can observe your thoughts, you understand that you are not them. That shift, subtle, almost invisible, is the birth of inner freedom.

From there, the practice becomes simple but profound- use thoughts as tools, not as masters. Let them serve awareness instead of hijacking it. When an anxious thought arises, instead of fighting it, listen to what it needs to teach. When a joyful thought appears, savor it, but don't cling. When an old memory returns, watch it without fear, it is merely a shadow seeking acknowledgment before fading.

In this way, thoughts begin to work for you. They become like skilled instruments in the hands of awareness, each playing its note, contributing to the symphony of growth. Anger gives you strength to protect what matters. Doubt sharpens discernment. Sadness softens pride. Joy reminds you of connection. Each thought, when understood, refines consciousness.

The trouble begins only when identification replaces observation. When you say, "I am angry," instead of "Anger is passing through me," you shrink the vast sky of being into a single cloud. The thought, which was meant to inform you, starts to define you. Awareness, which was meant to use thoughts, becomes used by them. Awakening is nothing more than reversing this relationship.

To use thoughts as instruments means to cultivate the space between them and you. That space is sacred. In that space, wisdom is born. Every spiritual practice, whether meditation, reflection, prayer, or stillness, is designed to widen this space. The wider it becomes, the clearer life feels. Reactions turn into responses; confusion turns into insight.

This awareness does not destroy thought, it purifies it. The same mind that once created fear now begins to create understanding. The same imagination that once built anxiety now builds beauty. Thought transforms from noise into intelligence. It becomes the voice of consciousness itself, guiding rather than disturbing.

Thoughts also carry creative energy. When aligned with awareness, they have the power to shape reality. This is not mystical, it is the natural law of focus. What you repeatedly think about with emotion begins to influence your actions, your choices, and even your physical body. When awareness steers thought, manifestation becomes natural and graceful. When thought runs without awareness, life becomes mechanical and reactive.

The difference between awakening and ordinary living lies in this- the awakened person thinks consciously; the unawakened one thinks compulsively. Conscious thought is like a deliberate stroke of a brush, it paints meaning. Compulsive thought is like a trembling hand, it smears everything it touches. Both use the same mind; only awareness decides the quality.

Over time, when you begin to watch your thoughts with compassion and not condemnation, they lose their heaviness. They start reflecting the intelligence of the soul rather than the noise of conditioning. The mind becomes a servant of awareness instead of its jailer. You can then use thought deliberately, to comfort, to clarify, to create, to heal. The mind becomes an ally in awakening.

It is also important to see that even silence is not the absence of thought but the maturity of it. In deep silence, thought still exists in seed form, pure potential waiting for direction. That is why the greatest thinkers, artists, and mystics all value silence. In that stillness, thoughts gather strength, clarity, and grace. They become instruments tuned to truth.

At this stage of understanding, you no longer wish to escape thought or transcend the mind. You begin to appreciate it as a divine tool of exploration. Consciousness uses thought the way a musician uses sound, to express the inexpressible. Every insight, every discovery, every act of compassion or creation begins as a single thought, born in the quiet depths of awareness.

The ultimate mastery, then, is not thoughtlessness but thought-clarity. It is not an empty mind, but a transparent one, where thoughts pass freely without residue. Such a mind is like a clear river- it moves, it reflects, it nourishes, and yet remains pure.

And perhaps this is the highest form of awakening, to realize that thoughts, too, are part of the divine design. They were never obstacles to enlightenment; they were its raw material. Fearful thoughts taught you courage. Painful thoughts taught you patience. Doubtful thoughts taught you discernment. Every thought, in its own way, has been leading you back to awareness.

When you finally see this, gratitude replaces resistance. You stop fighting your mind and start listening to it with reverence. The same thoughts that once imprisoned you now become your path to freedom. They are no longer random noises but notes of a sacred melody, one that has been playing since the beginning of time.

So let your thoughts come. Let them speak. But stay awake while they do. Use them as you would use any fine instrument, with attention, respect, and joy. And in that awareness, you will find what every seeker eventually discovers- that the mind, when understood, is not a problem to be solved, but a divine instrument through which consciousness learns to sing.

PART III
TRANSCENDING FEAR

8 THE MEANING OF SURRENDER

There comes a moment in every journey of awareness when knowledge reaches its limit. The mind, after years of analysis and effort, begins to see that no amount of control can guarantee peace. It has observed its own patterns, its fears, ambitions, victories, and defeats, and realizes that even the most brilliant plan cannot command life. What once felt like mastery now feels like restlessness. At that threshold, when intellect has exhausted itself, a new understanding begins to dawn. It is not born of thought, but of recognition. It whispers- Let go.

Surrender begins where resistance ends. It is not the act of giving up, it is the art of giving in. It is not failure to act, but freedom from forcing. It is the discovery that life moves with an intelligence far greater than the one we try to impose upon it. The river flows without needing to know where it ends; the seed sprouts without calculating its growth. Only the human mind, armed with reason but detached from trust, struggles against the current of existence.

To surrender is to return to alignment. It is to acknowledge that the same intelligence that turns night into day, that holds the stars in their orbits, that breathes through you without asking permission, also guides the events of your life. You are not separate from that rhythm, you are that rhythm, expressed in human form. The illusion of control is what creates friction; surrender restores harmony.

In the beginning, surrender feels frightening because it dismantles the ego's illusion of command. The mind has been trained to believe that safety lies in certainty and power lies in control. But the more it clings, the more it suffers, because control is an endless battle against the nature of change. Surrender is not a weakness in this battle; it is the moment you realize there was no battle at all. Life was never against you, it was only waiting for your cooperation.

When you surrender, you do not stop making choices; you stop making war with what already is. You still act, but the action flows from clarity, not compulsion. You still plan, but the plan no longer carries the anxiety of perfection. Surrender transforms doing into being, it turns effort into expression.

In the deeper sense, surrender is not something you decide to do; it is something that happens when you truly understand. When the mind finally sees the futility of resistance, surrender unfolds by itself, like a flower opening at dawn. It is the natural flowering of wisdom, the highest intelligence of consciousness.

The paradox is that surrender gives you more strength than control ever could. The controlled mind operates within its limited knowledge; the surrendered mind moves in harmony with infinite intelligence. The one who surrenders stops reacting and starts responding. They become flexible yet grounded, calm yet alive, strong yet compassionate. Surrender does not make you small, it makes you vast, because you stop defining yourself by boundaries.

Every teacher, every mystic, every enlightened being has spoken of surrender not as defeat but as culmination. It is the summit of awareness, the point where understanding ripens into trust. Through surrender, the separate self merges with the whole. The anxiety of "me" gives way to the peace of "we." The restless question "What will happen to me?" dissolves into the quiet knowing that whatever happens, happens through me, for me, and as me.

Surrender is the completion of intelligence because it unites the two halves of the human journey- knowledge and faith. Knowledge teaches us how life works; faith teaches us to trust that it does. When both come together, living becomes effortless. You do what you must, but you no longer carry the burden of outcome. You trust the process because you have seen its perfection in everything, from the sunrise to your own heartbeat.

This is the true meaning of surrender- to live intelligently enough to know that the greatest wisdom lies in trust. Not blind faith, not passive resignation, but a deep, clear cooperation with the unfolding of life. When you move with that rhythm, life stops being a struggle and becomes a dance.

The same energy that once expressed as fear now moves as faith; the same tension that once sought control now becomes creative flow. To surrender is to see that there was never anything to surrender to, because the divine you seek outside has always been the consciousness within. The one who lets go and the one who holds the universe together are not two. In that realization, the search ends, and peace begins.

Surrender as Highest Intelligence-

From childhood, most of us are taught that strength means control. We learn to push harder, plan smarter, and never yield. The idea of surrender is painted as failure, as if letting go means losing, or trusting means being naive. Yet, in truth, surrender is not the fall of intelligence; it is its flowering. It is not the collapse of will, but the alignment of will with wisdom.

The highest intelligence is not the one that controls the world; it is the one that understands it cannot. To surrender is to see reality as it is, not as we want it to be. It is the courage to stop arguing with what is. The mind that surrenders does not become passive, it becomes profoundly awake. It no longer wastes its energy resisting life; it uses that energy to respond to it.

Surrender is the point where understanding ripens into humility. It is the quiet realization that life, in all its complexity, is too vast to be managed by thought alone. The intellect is a wonderful tool, but it is not the author of existence. Every heartbeat, every breath, every turn of the earth happens without our command. The very fact that we are alive is proof that something beyond our control already sustains us. To surrender is to recognize that intelligence, not as a concept, but as a living presence guiding every moment.

When we surrender, we are not bowing to fate; we are returning to flow. The river that resists its course only creates turbulence. The river that flows freely reaches the ocean effortlessly. The same is true for the human mind. Resistance creates noise, surrender brings clarity. It replaces the anxious question "Why me?" with the peaceful statement "Let it be."

The ego fears surrender because it believes surrender will make it powerless. But in reality, surrender restores true power, the power that comes from alignment, not domination. The power that does not struggle, but acts with precision. The power that does not depend on force, but on awareness. When you surrender, you stop fighting the current of life and start moving with it. What once felt like chaos begins to feel like choreography.

Surrender does not mean you stop thinking or planning. It means your thoughts and plans no longer arise from fear. You still act, but your action is guided by clarity, not anxiety. You still strive, but your striving is joyful, not desperate. You work with full intensity, yet you remain inwardly relaxed. This combination of effort and ease is the signature of true surrender.

In a surrendered state, intelligence functions at its highest potential because it is no longer divided. The mind, heart, and body begin to move as one. The noise of resistance subsides, and intuition awakens. Insight comes effortlessly, creativity flows naturally, and decisions align with timing. You begin to experience what ancient wisdom always hinted at, that life supports those who cooperate with it.

To the ordinary mind, surrender looks like inaction. But to the awakened mind, it is the highest form of action, because it is action in harmony with truth. It is not about doing less, but about doing rightly. The surrendered person does not act from compulsion, but from connection. Their decisions arise not from panic or pressure, but from peace.

Every great discovery, every timeless work, every act of compassion has emerged from this surrendered intelligence. When the thinker stops struggling, insight arrives. When the artist stops striving, inspiration flows. When the heart stops controlling, love begins. The greatest achievements of humankind are not born from domination, but from attunement.

Surrender is not weakness, it is the end of inner conflict. Weakness fights reality; strength accepts it. Weakness clings to control; strength trusts connection. The one who resists may look strong, but inside they are tense and tired. The one who surrenders may appear still, but within them moves the quiet force of the universe.

Look at nature, it thrives on surrender. The flower opens to sunlight without anxiety. The bird trusts the air with its wings. The earth yields to rain and becomes fertile. Life itself is a continuous act of surrender, every moment arising and dissolving effortlessly into the next. Only the human mind resists, imagining itself as separate, special, or in charge. But even that resistance is part of the grand design, meant to teach us the futility of separation.

When the lesson is learned, surrender happens naturally. It is not a decision; it is an awakening. You suddenly realize that there is nothing to defend, nothing to prove, nothing to control. What you thought was your life is, in truth, life itself happening through you. The relief that follows this realization cannot be described, it must be experienced. It feels as though a great weight has fallen away, as though you have returned home after a long journey of pretending to be someone else.

Surrender gives birth to peace, but also to profound intelligence. The mind, once freed from constant control, becomes sharp and clear. Awareness expands. You start to see connections where before you saw conflicts. You begin to sense the invisible threads weaving everything together. It is as though existence begins to speak a language you can finally understand, a language of rhythm, patience, and precision.

This is why every spiritual tradition, in its own way, calls surrender the highest wisdom. Because it is not the end of understanding; it is the beginning of understanding without fear. It is the moment when the seeker stops seeking and starts trusting. It is the completion of evolution, not in the biological sense, but in the emotional and spiritual sense.

Surrender is not the death of individuality; it is the birth of authenticity. When you stop pretending to control everything, you start living truthfully. You stop chasing validation and start embodying presence. Life becomes simple again, not because problems disappear, but because your relationship with them changes. You no longer see challenges as threats, but as part of the dance of existence.

And here lies the paradox that completes the circle- the moment you surrender, you realize you were never separate to begin with. The same intelligence that guides the stars was guiding you all along. You were never the wave fighting the ocean, you were the ocean expressing itself as a wave.

To surrender, therefore, is not to lose, it is to remember. It is to remember that life is trustworthy, that intelligence pervades everything, that the universe is not random chaos but a living harmony. The one who truly surrenders does not fall; they finally rest in the hands that were carrying them all along.

Why Control Creates Fear-

Control is the mind's oldest defense. It begins in childhood, when uncertainty first feels unsafe. A child learns that if they can arrange their toys, their grades, or their parents' attention in a predictable order, the world feels less frightening. That instinct never really leaves us. As adults, we simply replace toys with titles, attention with approval, and still try to hold life steady through constant planning and mental rehearsal.

At first, control looks like intelligence in action. We plan our careers, save for the future, and try to keep everything "on track." But beneath that productivity often hides anxiety, a quiet tension that whispers, What if this doesn't go the way I expect? The more we try to control life, the more we notice how uncontrollable it is. Every attempt to fix the future makes the present heavier, because we keep measuring what is against what should be.

Control is born from fear, but ironically, it also feeds fear. When the mind insists that life must behave a certain way, every deviation feels like danger. The moment plans change, panic appears. The smallest obstacle feels like a threat to identity, because control has convinced us that stability equals safety, and instability equals loss. Yet life itself is movement, and movement means change. Trying to control that movement is like trying to keep a wave from rising and falling.

The desire for control comes from a misunderstanding of responsibility. We assume that to be responsible means to ensure outcomes. In truth, responsibility means responding, not guaranteeing. When we confuse the two, fear becomes our constant companion. We spend our days imagining all that could go wrong, building invisible cages around the future. The more we try to lock things into place, the less alive we feel.

The tragedy of control is subtle- it steals the joy of participation. When you're obsessed with steering, you stop seeing the scenery. When you're constantly predicting, you stop perceiving. Life becomes a series of rehearsals for a play that never quite happens, because you're too busy adjusting the script. The mind says, If I can just get this right, then I'll rest. But rest never comes, because the list of conditions never ends.

Fear thrives wherever control lives. Every "what if" thought is the child of control- What if I fail? What if I lose this job? What if they leave me? What if I fall ill? The mind keeps producing these because control depends on prediction, and prediction depends on fear. It needs fear to justify itself. Without fear, control loses purpose. So it keeps fear alive, feeding it small doses of uncertainty so it can stay in charge.

But life, being infinitely wiser, does not obey. It interrupts our plans with illness, detours, delays, and surprises, not as punishment, but as correction. It keeps reminding us that reality cannot be domesticated. The weather shifts, markets fall, people change, bodies age. These are not flaws in the system; they are the system. The more we resist them, the more disconnected we feel from the rhythm of existence.

Control narrows perception. It makes the world smaller and heavier. When we cling too tightly, our awareness contracts until we see only threats and tasks. But when control relaxes, attention expands. We begin to notice the subtleties, a conversation's warmth, the silence between words, the way life quietly supports us even when plans fail. In that expansion, fear loses its grip, because the unknown no longer feels like an enemy.

To surrender control does not mean abandoning order or discipline. It means exchanging rigidity for responsiveness. A dancer follows rhythm but does not force it; a sailor adjusts sails but cannot command the wind. The wise person acts in the same way, engaged, but not enslaved by expectation. They work with life, not against it.

The irony is that real control arises only after we stop trying to control everything. When the mind stops grasping, clarity returns. From that clarity, decisions become more accurate, not less. Because they're no longer distorted by fear, they arise naturally, like ripples on still water. Control built on fear makes us reactive; awareness built on trust makes us responsive.

One of the greatest sources of fear in modern life is the illusion that we can secure permanence. We build careers, accumulate wealth, or design routines not simply for comfort but to outsmart change itself. Yet every form eventually dissolves. What remains is the consciousness that witnesses it all, the awareness untouched by loss or gain. When we identify with that awareness instead of the outer forms, control loses its appeal, and peace quietly takes its place.

Surrender does not mean that we stop caring; it means we care without clinging. We still plan, but we accept that plans may evolve. We still love, but without the anxiety of possession. We still work, but with freedom from the tyranny of result. In this balance, life becomes light again. We no longer live as fearful managers of circumstance, but as participants in an unfolding intelligence that knows more than we ever could.

When you finally see that control cannot guarantee safety, you stop worshipping control. You start trusting presence instead. Presence is not the absence of action; it is the awareness that action happens through you, not from you. It is the moment you realize that your role is to respond, not to rule.

At that point, fear begins to fade, not because life becomes predictable, but because unpredictability no longer feels hostile. You start to see that what you once called chaos is actually creativity in motion. The future, once frightening, becomes open terrain. You stop bracing against life and start breathing with it.

The truth is simple- fear is not born from uncertainty; it is born from our refusal to be uncertain. Control is that refusal. The day we accept that uncertainty is the natural language of existence, fear loses its foundation. And in that acceptance, surrender ceases to look like weakness and begins to feel like wisdom.

Letting the Future Belong to the Divine-

The human mind is a magnificent instrument, capable of planning, predicting, and shaping the visible world. Yet, it is also haunted by its own limitations. It cannot see beyond the moment, but it keeps trying to. It cannot control the flow of time, but it keeps calculating it. This constant attempt to master the future is the root of inner exhaustion. The irony is that the more we try to secure tomorrow, the less we can enjoy today.

Surrender begins when we realize that the future was never meant to be owned. It was meant to unfold. Just as no gardener can force a seed to bloom on command, no person can command the rhythm of life. We can plant, nurture, and protect, but the blossoming is not ours to dictate. When we let the future belong to the Divine, or to the universal intelligence that orchestrates everything, we step out of fear and into flow.

Every culture, every philosophy, and every mystic tradition has, in its own words, hinted at this truth- life is not random, it is rhythmic. The same precision that turns the earth, that aligns the tides with the moon, that breathes through a sleeping infant, also governs the timing of our joys and sorrows. When we surrender to that rhythm, we are not giving up control, we are aligning with perfection that already exists.

To let the future belong to the Divine does not mean to sit idle or neglect responsibility. It means to act fully, but without anxiety. It means to give your best to the present moment and trust that the intelligence of the universe will take care of the rest. You plant your actions like seeds in fertile soil, with attention, care, and intention, but you do not pull the sapling every morning to check its growth. The surrender lies not in the planting, but in the patience.

The mind, however, resists this. It wants guarantees. It wants timelines, outcomes, and proofs. It keeps asking, "What if?" But the Divine never answers such questions with certainty, it answers with opportunities. The moment you stop demanding fixed answers, you start noticing quiet synchronicities, moments of right timing, unexpected help, invisible protection. These are the signatures of a higher intelligence at work, one that functions beyond human logic but always toward harmony.

When you truly let the future belong to that intelligence, fear begins to dissolve. You realize that even what seems like delay or loss has purpose. The job that didn't come, the plan that failed, the relationship that ended, all of these were silent adjustments, guiding you toward what was meant to grow instead. The future, then, is not a place to be controlled, but a mystery to be trusted.

To surrender the future is to stop living as a forecaster and start living as a participant. It is to let each day reveal itself like a page turning on its own, trusting that the story is being written with meaning, even when you cannot see the next chapter. You become less obsessed with "what's next" and more available to "what's now." And in that availability, the present becomes luminous. The mind that once lived ten steps ahead finally comes home to where life actually happens.

There is immense intelligence in uncertainty. It keeps us humble, curious, and alert. It is uncertainty that makes space for creativity, for discovery, for awe. If the future were predictable, life would lose its wonder. The Divine, in its subtle generosity, hides tomorrow not to punish us, but to protect us, to keep us engaged in the miracle of today.

When you surrender the future, even pain becomes sacred. You start to see how each event, pleasant or unpleasant, contributes to your unfolding. Fear transforms into trust, and trust transforms into gratitude. You stop seeing life as a series of tests and start recognizing it as a continuous teaching.

At that depth of surrender, a quiet confidence arises, not the confidence of knowing outcomes, but the confidence of knowing that you will be guided through them. This is a different kind of security, one not dependent on success or stability. It is the security of alignment, the feeling that no matter what happens, you are held within the same intelligence that moves galaxies and grows grass.

Those who have tasted this way of living describe it as lightness. They still plan, still dream, still act, but there is no tension behind their effort. Their decisions come from calm, their work from love, their rest from faith. They move through life not as controllers, but as co-creators. The difference is profound- the controller fears failure; the co-creator trusts timing.

The act of letting go does not make you powerless. It gives you a new kind of power, the power of participation in something vast and benevolent. You no longer feel alone in your efforts. You feel accompanied, guided. You begin to notice that life often helps those who trust it, in ways logic could never explain. The right people appear, the right opportunities arrive, and even setbacks redirect you with hidden purpose.

This is not magic; it is maturity. The maturity of a mind that finally understands that life's intelligence exceeds its own. The maturity of a heart that finally stops resisting and starts listening. The maturity of a being that knows, deeply, quietly, that the same force that has carried it through every past challenge will carry it through every future one.

When we let the future belong to the Divine, we step into a life of cooperation instead of competition, faith instead of fear. The storms may still come, but we stop fearing the rain, because we know it nourishes the soil of tomorrow. The road may still turn unexpectedly, but we stop panicking at the curves, because we trust the hands that built the road.

Surrendering the future is not an act of faith alone, it is the highest act of intelligence. It is the moment the mind recognizes its rightful place in the vastness of creation, not as a master, but as a partner. And when that understanding settles deeply, peace arrives not as a visitor but as a resident.

Trust in the Cosmic Order-

There is a moment, after the storms of resistance have passed, when silence begins to feel like truth. The mind that once wrestled with every detail of life grows tired of the endless struggle to arrange perfection, and in that weariness, a new stillness dawns. It is not indifference; it is understanding. It is the recognition that beneath all apparent chaos, there is rhythm, an intelligence older than thought, more trustworthy than effort. This is the peace that arises from trusting the cosmic order.

Everything in existence moves with purpose. The planets revolve in balance, tides follow lunar pulse, the heart beats without command. We rarely pause to marvel that the entire universe operates in harmony without a central controller shouting orders. The system sustains itself through equilibrium, not enforcement. Yet the human mind, small but ambitious, believes it must personally maintain this balance. It imagines itself as the architect of outcomes, the keeper of stability, and in doing so, it creates the only instability that truly exists- inner conflict.

Trust in the cosmic order is not blind faith; it is refined perception. It means seeing that the same intelligence that turns seasons, guides your own unfolding. It is the shift from believing in luck to recognizing pattern. When you look back at your life, the very events that once felt like misfortune often reveal themselves as necessary adjustments, a delay that protected you, a rejection that redirected you, a loss that cleansed you. What once looked random begins to look designed. That design is the language of the cosmos.

Peace begins when you stop demanding explanation and start practicing observation. The cosmic order does not owe you justification; it offers demonstration. Every sunrise is a reminder that endings lead to beginnings. Every night sky is proof that even darkness is filled with light if you know how to look. When the mind aligns with these truths, trust is not a decision, it is the natural fragrance of understanding.

To live in trust is to live in rhythm. You no longer panic when plans shift because you know movement is the law of life. You no longer cling to outcomes because you sense that what belongs to you cannot be lost, and what leaves you was never meant to stay. You still dream, still strive, still love, but you do it with openness rather than obsession. The difference is subtle yet transformative-tension turns into tenderness, ambition turns into alignment.

Trust restores proportion. It returns the human being to its rightful place within the universe, not as its master, but as its participant. In that participation, responsibility remains, but control dissolves. You still water the plant, but you no longer scold the clouds for not raining. You still work hard, but you no longer curse the timing of reward. You learn to play your part in the orchestra of existence without trying to conduct the entire symphony.

Fear cannot survive where trust lives. Fear thrives in the unknown; trust turns the unknown into sacred ground. To the fearful mind, uncertainty is danger. To the trusting mind, uncertainty is invitation, a chance to meet what you cannot predict but may still love. This shift changes everything- relationships soften, creativity deepens, and life stops feeling like a test you must pass and starts feeling like music you are meant to dance to.

Peace through trust is not a passive peace. It is vibrant, awake, and unshakable. It does not depend on stillness around you; it grows from stillness within you. When storms arrive, you no longer pray for the wind to stop, you remember you have roots. The tree does not fight the weather; it bends, and in bending, it survives. The same is true for a surrendered mind. It bends to circumstance, but it never breaks, because its strength comes from understanding, not from resistance.

This peace is not a reward given by fate; it is the essence of your own being uncovered. When you trust the order of existence, you stop living as a frightened fragment and start living as part of the whole. The separation between "me" and "life" dissolves. You no longer say, "Life is happening to me." You say, "Life is happening through me." That single shift of language reflects the greatest shift of consciousness, from struggle to participation, from fear to flow.

The cosmic order does not demand belief; it invites recognition. You can feel it in the timing of things, in the quiet intelligence behind coincidences, in the way lessons repeat until they're learned, in how love returns in new forms after loss. When you begin to see this design, trust becomes natural, and peace becomes inevitable. Not because you know what will happen, but because you know whatever happens will belong perfectly to the moment.

Peace through trust is the highest form of intelligence, because it arises from total understanding. The mind has seen enough to know that control fails; the heart has felt enough to know that life provides. Together they arrive at simplicity- do your best, and let life do the rest. What follows is not surrender in the sense of giving up, it is surrender in the sense of growing up. Maturity is not measured by how much we control, but by how gracefully we let go.

In that grace, life becomes gentle again. You notice beauty where before you saw burden. You meet uncertainty not with fear but with curiosity. You work, rest, speak, and love with equal presence. You become, in essence, a mirror of the universe itself, steady, spacious, and silent within movement.

This is the peace every seeker longs for, though most look for it in possession or success. Yet peace was never lost; it was only buried under resistance. The moment you trust the cosmic rhythm, resistance melts, and peace surfaces on its own, not as a visitor, but as your nature returning home.

9 THE SECOND PATH – CELEBRATIONS

There comes a stage in every seeker's journey when peace alone no longer feels complete. The silence that once healed the wounds of struggle now begins to whisper a new invitation, to live, to express, to rejoice. After the storm has settled and the waves have calmed, a quiet music rises from within, asking not for stillness anymore, but for movement. That music is celebration, the second path of awakening.

Surrender teaches you to let go; celebration teaches you to let flow. One ends resistance, the other begins resonance. To surrender is to find peace with life; to celebrate is to fall in love with it. Where surrender dissolves fear, celebration transforms it. It turns the raw energy of existence, joy, pain, loss, and wonder, into rhythm, movement, and grace.

Many believe that spiritual maturity means detachment, silence, and withdrawal from the noise of life. But true maturity is not retreat, it is participation without fear. It is to move through joy without losing balance and through sorrow without losing heart. It is to live with eyes open and arms wide, knowing that every experience, whether luminous or dark, is part of the same divine design.

Celebration is not about pleasure or entertainment; it is about awareness that has become musical. It is the dance of understanding, when you have seen that both laughter and tears are necessary instruments in the orchestra of existence. Celebration is the language through which the universe expresses its gratitude for being alive. When consciousness awakens, it does not reject life's dualities; it embraces them, and through that embrace, it begins to sing.

This world was never meant to be one-sided. The sun rises, and night returns. The tide moves in and out. Creation breathes through opposites, expansion and contraction, sound and silence, chaos and calm. Everything alive exists between these two poles, including the human heart. When we resist one side and cling to the other, we break the rhythm of existence and call it suffering. But when we move with both, we rediscover harmony.

The purpose of this chapter is not to teach escape from pain, but transformation through participation. When you celebrate life, you do not celebrate only what pleases you, you celebrate the entire play. The heart of a true celebrant knows that even sorrow is sacred, because it deepens love; even loss is holy, because it teaches presence. Celebration is not a denial of pain; it is the realization that pain, too, dances in the same circle as joy.

In celebration, the individual and the universe move together. There is no division between the dancer and the dance, between the singer and the song. You stop asking whether life is fair or unfair and begin to see that fairness was never the point, rhythm was. You stop chasing permanent happiness and begin to experience continuous aliveness. That shift, from seeking happiness to embodying aliveness, is the doorway to liberation.

To celebrate is to say yes to existence in its totality. It is to welcome each moment, not because it is easy or pleasant, but because it is real. It is to live without conditions, without fear, without complaint. You may cry, you may laugh, you may lose and gain, but through it all, a deeper current flows, whispering- This too belongs.

In the earlier chapters, surrender dissolved resistance by teaching you to trust the cosmic intelligence. Now, celebration expands that trust into joy. Where surrender says, *I* accept, celebration says, *I* participate. Surrender ends the conflict between you and life; celebration ends the distance. It is not enough to sit beside the river in peace, now you must swim in it, sing with it, and let it carry you.

When the mind no longer fears and the heart no longer clings, awareness becomes playful. That playfulness is not childishness; it is divine innocence, the capacity to engage with life without burden, without bitterness. It is the innocence that laughs even in uncertainty, that dances even with doubt.

The wise do not celebrate after life becomes perfect. They celebrate because it already is, in all its imperfection, all its contrast, all its beauty wrapped in chaos. They see that the universe does not need fixing; it needs participation. They do not pray for a different world; they bless this one by living it fully.

This is the second path, the path where peace blooms into joy, where awareness turns into song, and where the human spirit learns the most sacred truth of all- that life, even with its darkness, is worthy of celebration.

The Universe's Dual Pulse-

If you listen deeply to existence, you will hear that it breathes. Every wave that rises must fall; every night that descends must yield to dawn. The entire cosmos moves like a vast heartbeat, contracting, expanding, creating, dissolving. It is this continuous pulse that sustains life, this oscillation that gives meaning to stillness. Without darkness, light has no definition; without silence, music has no beauty; without loss, love has no value.

Everything that exists, exists in pairs. The human heart beats between systole and diastole, the earth spins between day and night, the ocean sways between tide and retreat. The universe itself is woven on the loom of opposites, and yet, these opposites are not enemies. They are partners in creation, complementing one another in a dance older than time.

We have been taught to chase only one side of this rhythm, to seek light and avoid shadow, to desire success and fear failure, to crave joy and escape sorrow. But such division is the birth of suffering. For the moment we reject one pole, we reject half of reality. And when we live in half of reality, the other half returns not as teacher, but as tormentor.

Look at nature, it holds no prejudice toward its seasons. Winter is not ashamed of its cold; summer is not proud of its warmth. Both serve the same purpose- the renewal of life. The tree does not curse autumn for taking its leaves; it simply stands in trust, knowing spring will return. The wise person lives like that tree, aware that life is not a straight line, but a circle.

Joy and sorrow, gain and loss, victory and defeat, these are not contradictions, they are continuations. Each flows naturally into the other, maintaining the balance of existence. If you were to take away sorrow, joy would vanish too, for joy derives its sweetness from the memory of pain. Gain means nothing without the experience of loss. Life's music depends on both the high and low notes; remove one, and the song collapses.

Our resistance to this duality is what exhausts us. We keep trying to make life one-sided, to fix it in perpetual daylight. But life does not tolerate stagnation. It changes because change is its nature. The universe is not a machine to be controlled; it is a melody to be joined. When you align with that melody, when you stop fighting the downbeat and start dancing with it, balance returns, and with it, peace.

When sorrow comes, it is not a punishment; it is the night restoring the balance of day. When loss arrives, it is not cruelty; it is space being cleared for a new beginning. Every downturn carries the seed of its opposite, waiting to unfold. This is the cosmic law, the rhythm that keeps creation alive.

There is a quiet intelligence in this rhythm. It does not waste energy on permanence, because permanence would mean death. It sustains life through movement, through endless giving and taking, expanding and contracting. The breath itself is the living proof- we inhale, we exhale. Try holding your breath, and even a few seconds of refusal turns the gift of life into struggle. The same happens when we hold on to joy or resist pain, we suffocate the flow of existence.

The dual pulse is not merely physical; it is psychological, emotional, spiritual. Within each person lives light and shadow, confidence and doubt, tenderness and anger. We are the microcosm of the same cosmic law. When you deny your sorrow, you deny your depth. When you suppress your fear, you suppress your courage. Awareness grows not by choosing one and rejecting the other, but by embracing both and seeing that they are not separate at all, they are phases of the same current of life.

There is beauty in knowing that you can survive both joy and sorrow, both abundance and absence. It gives birth to a calm strength, a strength that does not depend on constant sunshine. This strength is the essence of maturity. It knows how to smile even in the rain and how to rest even in uncertainty.

The spiritual mind does not escape polarity; it transcends it. Transcendence does not mean hovering above opposites, it means understanding them so completely that they lose their conflict. You begin to see that the sun and shadow both belong to the same light, that success and failure both serve the same evolution, that joy and sorrow are both gestures of love from the same source.

When you recognize this, life stops feeling unfair. You no longer see suffering as betrayal or joy as reward. You begin to sense that both are messages, the universe speaking two dialects of the same language. One whispers expansion, the other whispers humility. Together they teach wholeness.

It is this wholeness that turns life into celebration. You start to feel gratitude even for moments of pain, because they make your heart more receptive, more real. You see how contrast sharpens perception, how sadness deepens your compassion, how darkness teaches you to value light. You no longer live as a victim of duality; you become a student of rhythm.

The universe has never stopped dancing, and neither should you. The purpose of awakening is not to end the dance but to learn its steps, to move gracefully through the changes, trusting the unseen choreography. When you see the divine pulse behind all opposites, your resistance dissolves into wonder. You begin to celebrate not because everything is perfect, but because everything belongs.

This is the essence of the second path, to live in awareness of life's dual heartbeat and to find joy not in escaping its rhythm, but in moving with it. Once you realize that day and night are both sacred, that loss is the hidden face of gain, and that sorrow is love in another language, you have entered the true celebration of existence.

Accepting Both Halves of Creation-

To accept life is not to agree with everything that happens; it is to stop dividing the universe into things that should and should not be. The moment we decide that one half of creation is desirable and the other half is a mistake, we begin to live in conflict with the very order that sustains us. Acceptance does not weaken effort; it purifies it. It is the intelligence that allows you to act without hatred toward reality.

Every moment, existence offers two faces, gain and loss, health and sickness, praise and criticism. The untrained mind clings to one and curses the other. It says, I want light, but not shadow; success, but not failure; comfort, but not challenge. Yet the design of the world is not personal, it is cyclical. Refusing pain does not cancel it; it enlarges it, because resistance gives it permanence. Acceptance, on the other hand, allows movement. What is accepted passes through; what is resisted stays.

Acceptance is not resignation. Resignation says, Nothing can be done. Acceptance says, Something has been done by the whole, and I will flow with it until I see why. One closes the heart, the other opens it. In acceptance, the human being becomes transparent to life; events move through them like wind through an open window. This transparency is freedom, not because nothing touches you, but because everything touches you without leaving a scar.

We often imagine that peace means having only pleasant experiences. But peace grows from inclusion, not exclusion. The ocean is peaceful not because it is calm; it is peaceful because it can contain every storm. Similarly, a mature mind is not the one that avoids disturbance, but the one that can hold disturbance without drowning in it. Acceptance turns the mind into that vast ocean, it lets everything come and go without losing its depth.

The beauty of acceptance lies in the subtle transformation it brings. When you stop labeling an experience as enemy, it begins to reveal its teaching. Pain becomes depth, loss becomes clarity, failure becomes humility. Each so-called negative event carries a secret gift wrapped in discomfort. Only when you accept it does the wrapping open. Refusal keeps you busy fighting the package; acceptance lets you receive what is inside.

Acceptance also dissolves judgment toward others. Once you see that life operates in polarities, you stop demanding perfection from human beings who are also learning through opposites. You become kinder, because you know that everyone is wrestling with their own half of creation. Compassion arises naturally when comparison ends. The more you accept within yourself, the less you condemn outside yourself.

To accept both halves is to see the divine handwriting on every page. When joy visits, you bow in gratitude; when sorrow comes, you bow in recognition. The bow is the same. You do not prefer one guest over the other, because both are messengers of growth. In that even-handed bow lies a secret dignity, the quiet grace of a soul that has understood how the universe works.

The act of acceptance does not erase pain immediately; it erases its rebellion. After rebellion ends, pain softens on its own, because it no longer needs to shout to be heard. This is why acceptance feels lighter even in difficulty, it removes the extra weight of resistance. You begin to notice that peace was never about external order; it was always about internal allowance.

In the language of nature, everything accepts itself completely. The mountain does not wish to be a river; the river does not wish to be a cloud. Each form fulfills its role and then changes without complaint. Only the human mind argues with impermanence, demanding exceptions. Acceptance is simply returning to nature's intelligence, to know when to act and when to yield, when to hold and when to release.

Ultimately, acceptance is love in its most silent form. Love says yes to existence as it is. When that yes becomes steady, life stops feeling like an opponent and begins to feel like a companion. You no longer need to choose sides between light and dark, success and failure. You stand at the center, watching both move in harmony around you. In that center, celebration is born, not because life has become perfect, but because it has become whole.

Turning Fear into Rhythm, Pain into Participation-

There is a secret hidden in the rhythm of life- everything that frightens you contains a pulse, and everything that hurts you contains a lesson in movement. The same energy that trembles in fear can sing in freedom, if it is allowed to move. What traps most people is not fear itself, but their attempt to freeze it, to make it stop, to silence it, to make it disappear. Yet fear was never meant to be still; it was meant to flow.

Fear is life asking for attention. It is energy concentrated around uncertainty. When you suppress it, that energy hardens into anxiety; when you release it, it becomes alertness, awareness, and creative tension. The trembling that comes with fear is not weakness, it is the body's reminder that movement is the way out. Just as music releases emotion through vibration, awareness releases fear through rhythm.

To turn fear into rhythm is to let it teach you timing. Every pulse of fear asks, Are you present? It draws you back to the now, to the breath, the body, the heartbeat. The very sensations you once dreaded become instruments of awakening. Each wave of fear that you meet with awareness becomes part of the universal drumbeat, the same rhythm that moves tides and planets.

Pain, too, follows this law. When resisted, pain isolates; when participated in, it connects. To participate in pain does not mean to enjoy suffering; it means to stay conscious within it. Pain is the body's way of asking for presence; emotional pain is the soul's way of doing the same. When you sit with it, without dramatizing or fleeing, you discover that it begins to change texture, from solid to fluid, from unbearable to instructive.

There are two ways of dealing with pain- the way of avoidance and the way of participation. Avoidance says, This should not be happening. Participation says, This, too, is part of the dance. Avoidance turns you into a victim; participation turns you into a witness. The witness feels the pain fully yet remains untouched at the center, like the eye of a cyclone, calm amid all motion.

The mind that participates instead of resists becomes an alchemist. It takes every difficult emotion and converts it into understanding. Anger, when observed, becomes clarity about boundaries. Fear, when felt completely, becomes awareness of attachment. Loss, when embraced, becomes gratitude for what was given. Each feeling is energy wearing a temporary mask; participation is simply removing the mask and seeing the energy underneath.

To turn pain into participation is to realize that life does not happen *to* you; it happens *through* you. Every experience is a vibration moving through the instrument of your body and mind. When you let it move freely, the sound is music; when you block it, it becomes noise. The art of living lies in tuning yourself to this flow, allowing every experience, even the dissonant ones, to become part of a greater harmony.

Look at the ocean- even when storms churn its surface, the depth below remains serene. The waves do not fight the wind; they dance with it. The storm itself becomes part of the sea's expression. Likewise, when fear rises like wind and pain like rain, let them move. Let them pass through awareness instead of defining it. You are not the waves; you are the depth that allows them.

The mind fears pain because it imagines permanence. But no experience is permanent, every emotion, every thought, every loss has a life span. When you participate consciously, you see that even the deepest sorrow carries its own completion. Tears, when allowed, end. Fear, when faced, fades. What keeps pain alive is not its power but our refusal to listen.

Participation brings dignity to suffering. It transforms chaos into conversation. Instead of saying, Why me? you begin to ask, What is life showing me through this? That question opens a doorway, not out of pain, but through it. On the other side of that doorway lies compassion, wisdom, and humility.

Participation also reconnects you with others. When you have truly known pain without running, you can recognize it in another without judgment. You no longer pity or preach; you simply understand. That understanding is love in its purest form, the quiet acknowledgment that every being is learning the same rhythm in different steps.

The courage to participate is the foundation of celebration. Celebration is not the denial of pain; it is its transcendence. It is the moment you realize that even your scars are part of the design, that nothing has been wasted. The cracks in the heart are where the light of awareness enters. Once you see that, pain loses its poison and becomes power.

When fear transforms into rhythm, you no longer shake in terror, you move with grace. When pain turns into participation, you no longer ask for escape, you ask for understanding. That understanding turns life itself into a dance floor, every challenge a step, every emotion a note.

This is the heart of the second path- not to flee from life's intensity but to use it as music. To let every rise and fall of emotion remind you that you are part of the universe's grand choreography. The same rhythm that beats in your heart beats in the stars. The same pulse that moves through your fears moves through galaxies.

When you can dance with your fears, you have already conquered them. When you can participate in your pain, you are already healed. And when you can celebrate both equally, light and shadow, joy and ache, you are no longer a separate observer of life; you have become life itself.

The Sacred Art of Participation-

There is a profound difference between observing life and participating in it. Observation gives understanding, but participation gives belonging. When you observe, you remain a visitor; when you participate, you become part of the rhythm itself. The one who celebrates life does not stand on the shore watching the waves; they step into the tide, feeling its cool resistance, trusting its pull, knowing it will never drown what moves with it.

To live is to participate. Existence does not ask for perfection; it asks for presence. Every leaf that falls, every breath that passes, every moment that blooms and dissolves is an invitation to be here, not in theory, not in control, but in surrendering presence. The river of time flows whether you resist or not. Participation is the choice to swim with open eyes, to let life touch you completely, even when it stings.

This participation is sacred because it transforms everything it touches. It turns fear into depth, pain into insight, and joy into gratitude. The mind that participates in life no longer divides experiences into good and bad; it receives them as different tones of the same song. You begin to understand that life's purpose is not comfort, but completeness. Existence itself is an art, and the artist is not one who paints only with bright colors, but one who uses every shade, including the dark ones, to reveal wholeness.

Celebration is not the denial of darkness; it is the inclusion of it. The candle does not argue with the night; it simply shines, and in shining, it honors both light and shadow. When you celebrate life, you become that candle, aware of the darkness but no longer afraid of it. You understand that contrast gives meaning to beauty, and pain gives depth to love.

Participation ends separation. You no longer feel like a stranger in your own life. The sense of "me" and "the world," "my plan" and "God's plan," slowly merges into one seamless unfolding. You act, but not as a controller, as a conduit. You love, but not out of need, out of abundance. You live, but without clinging, because you trust that every movement, every moment, is perfectly placed within the cosmic rhythm.

When you participate consciously, the smallest actions become holy. Making tea, speaking gently, working, resting, even breathing, all become expressions of the same intelligence that spins the stars. You stop chasing meaning because you realize you are meaning in motion.

This is the sacred art of participation- to live so fully that even your silence is alive. It is to wake each morning not asking what life owes you, but what melody you can add to its song today. It is to walk through the world not trying to fix it, but to feel it, completely, deeply, lovingly.

To participate is to accept the invitation of existence, to dance while the music lasts, to bow when it ends, and to trust that another song will begin. For the one who lives in this way, fear no longer finds space to settle. There is no room for it in a heart that is too busy celebrating.

In the end, participation is not something you do; it is something you become. You become the dance you once feared to join, the light you once sought outside, the rhythm you once resisted. And when that happens, you realize the truth that sages have whispered across ages- life was never against you, it was only waiting for you to join in

10 THE DIVINE BALANCE

There is a law that governs both galaxies and human hearts, the law of balance. Everything that lives moves between two poles, seeking equilibrium- inhalation and exhalation, tension and release, joy and sorrow. When this movement flows freely, there is harmony. When it becomes fixed at one end, too much excitement, too much fear, too much desire, the current of life turns turbulent, and the mind calls it suffering.

Human beings are the meeting point of two universes- the physical and the subtle. The body belongs to the earth; the consciousness belongs to infinity. Between the two runs an invisible bridge, the breath. Each breath is a miniature version of creation- the in-breath gathers, the out-breath lets go. If we could hear carefully, we would notice that this rhythm mirrors the spinning of planets and the expansion and contraction of stars. Through this breath, the cosmos speaks to us in the language of energy.

Emotions are the tides of this inner ocean. They rise and fall according to the pull of countless forces, our thoughts, our chemistry, the subtle play of planetary fields, and the unbroken rhythm of cosmic motion. None of these forces are enemies. They are signals, not punishments. The sadness that slows you down, the joy that lifts you, the fear that sharpens your senses, all are expressions of the same divine intelligence adjusting the balance of your being. To reject them is to reject your own alignment.

The trouble begins when we mistake movement for malfunction. When joy comes, we cling to it; when sorrow visits, we resist it. Both reactions break the natural flow. The result is tension, the tightening of awareness that becomes stress, anxiety, and despair. Yet the emotion itself was never harmful; it was the body's attempt to recalibrate. Just as the heart quickens to supply oxygen in danger, the mind stirs emotion to restore harmony when awareness drifts. Fear, anger, or fatigue are not flaws; they are messages that say, return to balance.

From a spiritual view, even imbalance serves a sacred purpose- it reveals where consciousness is asleep. Every excess, of pleasure, ambition, or control, is a mirror showing us where we have forgotten the center. The divine design ensures that imbalance never lasts; sooner or later, life corrects itself. Storms pass, moods shift, bodies heal. The cosmos continuously re-balances its own creation. Our suffering is often nothing more than impatience with this natural correction.

When you see this pattern clearly, emotions stop being moral questions. Happiness and sadness lose their labels of good and bad. They become movements of the same energy, shaped by different notes in time. You begin to realize that you are not your emotions; you are the awareness through which they flow. In that realization, control gives way to cooperation, and resistance softens into rhythm.

Balance, then, is not achieved by suppressing emotion but by allowing every emotion its rightful place and proportion. To laugh when joy rises, to weep when tears come, to rest when fatigue whispers, this is intelligence, not weakness. Balance is not about staying still; it is about staying centered while everything moves. It is the still axis around which the wheel of life spins.

The Divine Balance is not something you must create; it is already happening. Every heartbeat, every breath, every cycle of sleep and wakefulness is evidence of it. All that is required is awareness, to notice the rhythm instead of trying to rewrite it. The more you recognize this, the less life feels like chaos and the more it feels like choreography.

This chapter explores that sacred choreography. It invites you to meet fear as a teacher, to see every emotion as one energy in motion, and to move from resistance toward rhythm and realization. For when balance is understood as divine, every rise and fall becomes holy, every experience becomes instruction, and peace is no longer a goal to reach but the natural state of a mind in harmony with the cosmos.

Fear as Teacher-

For centuries, fear has been branded the villain of human experience. It is blamed for hesitation, failure, and weakness. We are told to "conquer" it, to "overcome" it, as though fear were a foreign invader rather than a native voice. Yet if creation is intelligent, if nothing in existence is accidental, then fear, too, must serve a purpose. The question is not how to destroy fear, but how to understand what it is trying to teach.

Every emotion in the human spectrum exists for balance. Joy expands consciousness outward; fear draws it inward. Joy connects; fear protects. Without fear, we would walk into fire, touch the edge of cliffs, and ignore danger. It is the guardian of awareness, the silent intelligence that warns when boundaries are threatened. Nature never intended fear to be punishment; it designed it as preservation. It is the pause that precedes reflection, the contraction that saves the organism before expansion begins again.

What turned this natural reflex into an inner torment was not the feeling itself but our misunderstanding of it. When fear appears, we panic about panic. We add thought to sensation, Why am I afraid? What if this never ends? What will others think? The secondary storm of interpretation multiplies the original wave. In animals, fear lasts seconds- they freeze, assess, act, and move on. In humans, it can last years, replaying endlessly in imagination. The problem is not biology but belief.

To see fear rightly, one must first observe its anatomy. At the physical level, fear is energy, electrical impulses activating the amygdala, quickening the pulse, sharpening the senses. At the psychological level, it is focus, the mind narrowing attention to what seems most important. And at the spiritual level, it is awakening, life's way of reminding you that something unconscious seeks your care. When these three levels work together, fear becomes wisdom. When they clash, fear becomes suffering.

Imagine standing before a vast ocean. The first wave of fear is instinctive, the body recognizes depth, motion, and uncertainty. But if you breathe and watch, the same wave becomes awe. You begin to sense that fear and wonder are twins-both arise before the unknown. The difference lies in interpretation. Fear says, This is bigger than me; I might die. Wonder says, This is bigger than me; let me listen. The energy is identical; only the direction of attention changes.

When fear is met with awareness instead of resistance, its language becomes clear. It tells you where you have placed your false security. Fear of loss teaches attachment; fear of rejection teaches dependence; fear of failure teaches identification with outcome. Each fear points to a lesson in freedom. The moment you see the lesson, fear softens, its job is complete. Like a teacher who no longer needs to shout once the student understands, fear fades when learning begins.

At times, fear also appears as the messenger of timing. It slows action not to hinder progress but to prevent haste. Life often pauses us through fear when the ground ahead is not yet ready. What we call delay may simply be protection. The instinct to "wait" that arises from subtle anxiety can sometimes be the body's wisdom sensing what the intellect has not yet noticed. Listening to that wisdom is not weakness; it is collaboration with life's intelligence.

The ancient sages observed this intimately. They noticed that fear and breath were inseparable, every emotion altered the rhythm of breathing, and every conscious breath could alter emotion. They taught that breath is the bridge between body and cosmos, and that fear is the tightening of that bridge. When one breathes slowly and deeply, the bridge expands again, and fear dissolves into flow. Modern neuroscience now echoes this truth- controlled breathing calms the amygdala, balances the nervous system, and restores clarity. The body's design confirms the cosmos's design, rhythm restores balance.

But fear's role extends beyond biology. It shapes moral intelligence. Without fear of consequence, compassion would fade. The awareness that actions have impact, that life is interwoven, arises partly from this subtle vibration of fear, not terror, but reverence. The wise fear hurting others, wasting time, or betraying truth. Such fear does not shrink the heart; it refines it. It becomes conscience. The difference between sacred fear and crippling fear is consciousness. One binds; the other guides.

If we could look closely at moments of great transformation, an artist before the blank canvas, a scientist on the verge of discovery, a parent releasing a child into the world, we would see fear standing quietly beside love. Fear is always present where something important is at stake. It is the shadow of meaning. Only those who care deeply can feel deeply afraid. To banish fear entirely would be to banish significance itself. Life without fear would be mechanical, not miraculous.

The task, then, is not to erase fear but to refine relationship with it. When fear comes, do not ask, How do I get rid of you? Ask, What do you want me to see? This shift changes everything. Suddenly fear stops being an obstacle and becomes orientation. It points you toward growth, showing where courage must rise, where trust must deepen, where attachment must loosen. The same force that once froze you becomes the wind that propels you forward.

Every spiritual tradition that truly understands the human heart speaks of this transformation. In one language it is called surrender, in another mindfulness, in another faith. The surface rituals differ, but the essence is identical- look directly at what frightens you until it turns transparent. What remains is energy, pure, neutral, luminous. That energy, once freed from the label "fear," becomes awareness itself. The student has become the teacher.

This realization does not come all at once. It begins in small acts of attention. You notice the flutter in the stomach before a new beginning and breathe through it. You feel the tension before a conversation and stay present. You sense the trembling before loss and allow it to move instead of harden. Slowly, you start to trust fear's rhythm. You see that it rises, peaks, and falls like waves, leaving behind clarity, humility, and strength.

In that understanding, fear loses its drama. It becomes one more current in the great river of energy that is your life. Sometimes it comes to sharpen your vision; sometimes to slow your pace; sometimes simply to remind you that you are alive. When you stop labeling it enemy, it stops behaving like one. You realize that fear has been your oldest companion, following you from the first breath, protecting, warning, teaching, misunderstood, but never malicious.

The divine balance of creation could not exist without this energy. Just as gravity keeps planets in orbit, fear keeps consciousness anchored to awareness. Joy alone would scatter us into recklessness; fear alone would paralyze us. Together, they create rhythm, expansion and contraction, the breath of existence. To live in balance is not to silence fear but to let it harmonize with love, each completing the other's note.

When you see fear as teacher, gratitude arises naturally. You no longer curse the tremor before change; you bow to it. You understand that every trembling was preparation for awakening. The mind that once said, I must be fearless now says, I must be fully alive. And to be fully alive is to welcome every pulse of life, even the one called fear.

All as One Energy in Motion-

If one could step outside the frame of a single moment and see life as a whole, it would appear not as a sequence of events but as a single, flowing motion, like the ocean rising and falling in endless shapes. What we call emotions are merely waves upon that ocean. They rise, peak, and dissolve, yet the water beneath them never changes. The tragedy of human perception is that we mistake the wave for the water; we believe each feeling is separate, personal, and final. In truth, all experience, joy, grief, love, fear, calm, is energy taking different forms in motion.

The universe itself is movement. Nothing in existence stands still. Stars expand and collapse, tides advance and retreat, breath enters and leaves. Even what seems solid, the mountain, the stone, the body, is vibration condensed into form. Within this vast choreography, the mind is both observer and participant. It translates the movement of energy into sensation, the sensation into emotion, and the emotion into story. But the essence remains one- energy seeking harmony.

When the energy flows freely through us, we call it peace. When it meets resistance, we call it pain. The emotion itself is neutral; it is the movement that gives it color. Imagine a violin string, if tuned perfectly, its vibration creates music; if stretched too tight or left too loose, it creates noise. Emotions are the vibrations of consciousness; balance tunes them into harmony. A human life, when lived in awareness, becomes a symphony of these vibrations, sometimes soft, sometimes stormy, but always part of the same music.

Modern science too reveals this truth in its own language. Neurochemistry shows that every emotion corresponds to a pattern of electrical and hormonal activity, shifts in serotonin, dopamine, cortisol. The same molecule that carries excitement can, in another context, carry anxiety.

The difference is not chemical but contextual, how the brain interprets energy. Spiritual wisdom and science meet here- what we feel is not the event itself but our resonance with it. Emotion is energy translated through awareness.

This realization changes how we live. We begin to see that anger is not evil; it is energy misdirected. Sadness is not failure; it is love slowed down. Even numbness, the absence of feeling, is energy conserving itself. Each emotion is a messenger delivering information about the flow within. When we stop judging and start listening, we discover that all emotions belong to the same river, and that river is sacred.

Breath is the bridge through which we experience this unity. Each inhalation draws in energy; each exhalation releases it. When breath flows easily, emotions flow with it. When breath tightens, emotions stagnate. The rhythm of breathing mirrors the rhythm of existence, day and night, tides, seasons, the heart's own pulse. That is why ancient teachers said that mastering the breath is mastering life itself. They were not speaking metaphorically; they meant that awareness of breath reconnects you with the universal rhythm.

If you observe closely, you will see that emotion moves through the body like weather through the sky. A thought triggers a feeling, the feeling stirs the heart, the heart alters the breath, and the breath shapes the body's posture. The body and mind are not two separate systems but two ends of one circuit. When you relax the body, the mind softens; when you calm the mind, the body releases. Awareness unites them both in motion. This is why meditation, dance, art, music, and even silent contemplation bring relief, they allow energy to move again.

The misunderstanding of emotion as fixed identity is what traps people in cycles of suffering. We say, "I am angry," instead of, "Anger is passing through me." The first statement builds walls; the second opens doors. The first breeds guilt or pride; the second invites curiosity. When you identify with an emotion, you freeze it; when you witness it, you free it. The difference between imprisonment and liberation lies in a single shift, from ownership to observation.

Every experience, even painful ones, has a natural completion built into it. If left unhindered, energy resolves itself, tears wash grief, laughter releases tension, silence absorbs confusion. Problems arise when we interrupt this cycle by suppressing or exaggerating feelings. Suppression blocks energy; exaggeration distorts it. Both create imbalance.

The art of balance is the art of letting emotion move through its full arc without interference, neither pushing it away nor pulling it closer. Like allowing the tide to come and go, knowing the ocean remains full regardless.

To live in this awareness is to see beauty in everything, even in contrast. The night does not oppose the day; it completes it. The valley gives meaning to the mountain. Likewise, sadness gives depth to joy, and fear gives edge to courage. They are not enemies but partners in rhythm. Without one, the other loses meaning. The divine design thrives on polarity because polarity creates motion, and motion sustains life.

Once you perceive this unity, your relationship with experience transforms. Instead of labeling emotions as good or bad, you begin to ask, What is this energy inviting me to learn? Sometimes the invitation is to rest; sometimes to act; sometimes simply to witness. In all cases, the invitation is toward balance. You no longer chase happiness or run from sadness; you flow with both. The pursuit ends, and peace begins, not the peace of stillness, but the peace of participation.

There comes a moment, through this practice, when even language begins to feel unnecessary. The mind grows quiet, the breath gentle, and life seems to move of its own accord. You watch joy arise and fade, fear appear and dissolve, without resistance. You realize that you are not the dancer but the dance itself, the rhythm moving through every cell. This is what mystics meant when they said, "The drop knows itself as the ocean." You are not feeling emotions; life is feeling itself through you.

This understanding does not make you indifferent; it makes you intimate with everything. You cry more deeply, laugh more freely, love more sincerely, because nothing threatens you anymore. You see that joy and sorrow are not opposites but reflections. Each moment is a wave, and you are the sea. The awareness of this truth is the beginning of freedom. It is what turns living from survival into art.

So the next time emotion rises, whether fear, anger, longing, or bliss, do not rush to label it or fix it. Pause. Feel its rhythm. Watch how it moves through breath, thought, and body. Notice that beneath its movement lies a stillness untouched. That stillness is what you truly are, and the motion upon it is how life expresses itself. To live this way is to live in balance- dancing with energy without being drowned by it, feeling everything without being defined by anything.

When one truly understands that all experience is energy in motion, fear loses its sharpness, sorrow its heaviness, joy its urgency. They all become music, part of the same eternal composition. You stop trying to control the notes and start listening to the melody. That melody is life itself, singing through you, around you, and as you.

From Resistance → Rhythm → Realization-

Life does not begin with control; it begins with movement. Everything that exists is part of a rhythm older than thought, the pulse of expansion and contraction that sustains the entire cosmos. To live in harmony with this rhythm is to live in grace. To resist it is to suffer. Resistance is not sin; it is misunderstanding, the mind's attempt to oppose what it cannot yet comprehend. Yet the miracle of existence is that even resistance, when seen with awareness, becomes the first step toward realization.

The Nature of Resistance-

Resistance is the friction between what is and what we wish to be. It arises whenever the flow of reality meets the boundaries of expectation. You feel it when plans collapse, when people behave unpredictably, when change disrupts your comfort. At that moment, the mind tightens its grip on control. It begins to say, this should not be happening. That single thought, repeated, defended, and believed, becomes the seed of suffering.

But resistance itself is not the enemy. It is a signal, an early alarm that your inner rhythm has fallen out of sync with life's rhythm. Like a discordant note in a symphony, it draws your attention to what needs tuning. Every wave of anger, impatience, or fear is an invitation to listen more deeply. The universe does not punish; it corrects. Resistance is how correction begins.

Observe nature- no storm lasts forever, no tide resists its own ebb. Movement is the essence of life. Only the human mind, with its gift of imagination, tries to halt the flow. We say, "I want this feeling to stay forever," or "I never want this to happen again." Both statements reject reality's motion. And so, the natural current of life, which was meant to carry us, becomes the very thing we fight against.

The Weight of Control-

The more one resists, the heavier life becomes. Control, born from fear, breeds exhaustion. We try to manage not just circumstances but emotions, people, and even destiny. We plan endlessly, rehearse every conversation, worry about outcomes we cannot predict. This habit may appear as responsibility, but it is often resistance wearing a polite disguise.

The irony is that the more we seek control, the less control we feel. Every moment becomes a negotiation with uncertainty. The heart grows weary, the mind restless, the body tense. Sleep becomes shallow; joy becomes conditional. Life shrinks to the size of our plans. The grand symphony of existence becomes a single anxious note.

Control is not mastery; it is mistrust. It assumes that life cannot be trusted to unfold intelligently. Yet look closely at creation, galaxies spin without supervision, forests regenerate without management, rivers find their way without maps. The same intelligence that moves planets also moves within us. To resist it is to distrust our own essence. To surrender to it is not to give up, but to grow up, to mature beyond the illusion that we must govern what the divine already governs perfectly.

When Awareness Begins-

The transformation from resistance to rhythm begins the moment we pause. Awareness interrupts the automatic reflex to fight or flee. It allows a gap, a sacred stillness in which we can witness what is happening rather than react to it. That single pause is not small; it is the birth of freedom.

In that pause, you might notice that what you called suffering is actually movement, energy asking to flow. The tightness in the chest, the restlessness in the stomach, the tremor in the hands, all are waves waiting for release. The body knows what the mind has forgotten- that release, not repression, restores balance. Crying, laughing, breathing, walking, all are ways energy completes its cycle.

Awareness does not mean indifference. It means intimacy without interference. You feel fully but no longer drown. You observe the emotion as part of the larger rhythm, the same rhythm that moves clouds, tides, and breath. Slowly, awareness re-educates the nervous system. The body learns that it can feel intensity without collapsing. Fear softens, pain loosens, and the flow returns. This is rhythm, not the absence of challenge, but the presence of flow.

The Emergence of Rhythm-

Rhythm is the body's language for balance. Every heartbeat, breath, and neural pulse is part of an ancient choreography. When life becomes too rigid, rhythm dissolves; when we relax into presence, rhythm returns. You can sense this even in simple acts, walking mindfully, speaking from stillness, eating slowly, or listening completely. Each act becomes music when performed with awareness.

Rhythm does not mean predictability; it means participation. The dancer does not know every step in advance; she follows the beat as it unfolds. Similarly, to live rhythmically is to respond to life moment by moment, to let the inner pulse synchronize with the outer pulse. Plans remain, but they no longer imprison. You act, you adjust, you allow. Action becomes aligned with timing, not tension.

This is why people often find peace in nature or art. A forest has rhythm; it breathes. Music, dance, poetry, they all remind us of this flow. They move energy that words cannot. In rhythm, mind and body reconcile. The need to control gives way to curiosity. The energy once trapped in resistance begins to circulate again as creativity, vitality, love. What was once chaos now feels like choreography.

The Dance of Acceptance-

Acceptance is not passive. It is the most dynamic act of intelligence. It says, "This too belongs." When you accept what arises, joy or pain, gain or loss, you rejoin the rhythm of the cosmos. Acceptance does not change the event; it changes the relationship with the event. The same storm that once felt destructive now feels cleansing. The same silence that felt empty now feels full.

This acceptance is not resignation. It is trust in motion, trust that life's intelligence exceeds personal preference. It is like stepping into a river and realizing you do not have to carry the water; you have to let it carry you. Once this trust matures, even difficulty becomes dance. You may stumble, but you no longer fall. You move with life, not against it.

From Rhythm to Realization-

Rhythm gradually opens the mind to a deeper revelation- there is no "you" separate from the movement. The dancer and the dance are one. What you called my life is life itself unfolding through your form. This is realization, not an intellectual idea, but a direct knowing that everything is part of a single, living intelligence.

In realization, resistance has no foothold. The question "Why is this happening to me?" dissolves, because there is no "me" apart from what is happening. The question turns into wonder- "How beautifully this is moving through me." The same pain that once felt unbearable becomes tender; the same uncertainty that once felt terrifying becomes sacred. You realize that life was never against you, it was trying to include you in its rhythm all along.

Realization also reveals that peace is not the absence of movement but the awareness within it. The waves never stop, but you no longer mistake yourself for the wave. You are the ocean, watching your own motion. In that seeing, compassion blossoms naturally, for yourself, for others, for the whole creation. You understand that everyone is learning the same dance at their own pace.

The Role of Breath and Awareness-

The simplest key to maintaining rhythm and realization is breath. The breath is life's metronome, the pulse that keeps awareness anchored in the present. When you breathe consciously, you align with the universe's own timing. Each inhale reminds you that you are receiving; each exhale reminds you to release. Awareness follows this rhythm and begins to dissolve resistance at its root.

Try noticing how every emotion has a unique breath pattern- anger shortens it, fear freezes it, sadness deepens it. By consciously restoring the rhythm of breath, you allow the emotion to complete its course. You do not need to "fix" the feeling; you need to let it move. Breath is not merely physiological, it is metaphysical. It synchronizes your little rhythm with the universal rhythm. In that alignment, peace arises effortlessly.

Realization in Everyday Life-

Realization does not make you otherworldly; it makes you deeply human. It shows you that life's purpose is not to escape experience but to experience it consciously. Eating, working, loving, resting, all become expressions of balance. You still face challenges, but you no longer collapse into them. You respond instead of react. Each difficulty becomes a reminder to return to rhythm.

This awareness gradually dissolves the boundaries between the sacred and the ordinary. Washing dishes, driving through traffic, listening to rain, all become meditation. You begin to sense that divinity is not elsewhere; it is right here, pulsing through everything. Resistance fades, not because life became easier, but because you stopped insisting it should be different. What remains is simplicity, life as it is, and you as its witness.

The Grace of Impermanence-

In the end, realization brings a gentle truth- nothing is permanent, and that is beautiful. If every experience is energy in motion, then change is the heartbeat of existence. The attempt to make anything last forever, success, pleasure, even peace, creates stagnation. Letting go allows renewal. Like seasons, emotions and circumstances must change so that consciousness keeps evolving. The mature mind does not fear impermanence; it reveres it as grace.

Impermanence is the universe's way of ensuring participation. It prevents the heart from hardening and the mind from fossilizing. Each ending invites a new beginning; each loss prepares space for something higher. In the rhythm of gain and loss, you begin to sense a design that is both tender and wise. The one who once fought against change now bows before it, whispering, Thank you for keeping me alive.

Living the Realization-

To live this realization is to live lightly. You act fully but carry nothing. You feel deeply but cling to nothing. You trust the rhythm more than your preferences. You know that storms will come and pass, that joy will rise and fall, and that through it all you remain untouched, the silent witness behind the movement. This is freedom, not the freedom to control life, but the freedom to dance with it.

When you live like this, your presence itself becomes medicine. People around you sense calm without you preaching peace. They feel understood without you offering advice. Because you no longer resist, you radiate acceptance, and acceptance heals. You become the still center in the motion of others, reminding them, wordlessly, of their own rhythm.

The Circle Completes-

Resistance gave birth to seeking, seeking discovered rhythm, and rhythm revealed realization. The journey was never about becoming something else but remembering what you already are, an expression of the cosmic pulse. Every challenge, every fear, every moment of chaos was part of that remembering. The divine balance does not eliminate contrast; it integrates it. Sorrow and joy, fear and faith, all belong to the same circle. The circle was never broken; we simply forgot that we were spinning within it.

In the end, realization is not an achievement. It is a return, a return to simplicity, to participation, to gratitude. You no longer stand apart from life, analyzing it; you stand within it, aware. The heart beats, the breath flows, the world turns, and you realize that this motion, this endless rhythm, is love itself.

11 THE ART OF LIVING FEARLESSLY

Fearlessness is not a state of armor; it is a state of openness. It does not arrive when all danger is gone but when understanding dawns. To live fearlessly is not to become hard or unshakable, it is to become undefended, to stand in the middle of life's uncertainties with a quiet heart that knows, whatever comes, I will meet it fully.

The common idea of fearlessness has always been slightly mistaken. We imagine warriors charging into battle, leaders defying odds, heroes suppressing tremor and doubt. But true fearlessness is far more subtle. It does not roar; it breathes. It is not the end of fear but the beginning of wisdom. It is the flowering of a mind that has seen through fear's illusion and found peace not beyond it, but within it.

When one understands that fear is simply energy, the body's way of protecting what it loves, the war ends. You stop fighting fear and begin listening to it. You see that courage is not the absence of trembling but the willingness to walk while trembling. In that moment, a profound shift happens- fear transforms into alertness, alertness into awareness, and awareness into grace.

Fearlessness is not born in certainty; it is born in trust. Trust that life knows what it is doing. Trust that even when the path seems unclear, it is still guided by an intelligence deeper than the mind. This trust does not make you passive; it makes you calm. It allows you to move through life's chaos with dignity, to speak truth without hostility, to act without anxiety, to rest without guilt.

The fearless person does not avoid emotion; they embrace it without becoming its prisoner. They feel everything, joy and pain, gain and loss, but their center remains steady. Their stillness is not lifeless; it is alive with awareness. They have discovered that freedom lies not in escaping storms but in learning to dance in the rain.

To live fearlessly, then, is to live consciously. It is to see every moment as an invitation rather than a threat. It is to meet change without clinging, failure without collapse, and success without arrogance. It is to look at life and say, I am willing.

Willing to grow.
Willing to feel.
Willing to let go.

This chapter is not about becoming fearless; it is about remembering that you already are. Beneath layers of conditioning and control lies a natural strength, quiet, compassionate, unshakable. Fearlessness is simply the rediscovery of that original state. It does not need to be built; it needs to be uncovered.

When fear arises again, and it will, you will no longer see it as an intruder but as a reminder. A reminder to pause, to breathe, to trust the rhythm of existence. That rhythm has carried stars through darkness, waves through storms, and hearts through heartbreaks. It will carry you too.

This is the art of living fearlessly, not a technique or philosophy, but a way of being. A life lived in full participation with every experience, neither escaping nor clinging, only flowing, gently, intelligently, completely.

The Misunderstood Meaning of Fearlessness-

For most of human history, fearlessness has been portrayed as a conquest, a battle of the brave against the trembling heart. Stories, myths, and movies have trained us to believe that to be fearless is to suppress emotion, silence doubt, and walk through danger untouched. Heroes were admired not because they felt fear, but because they appeared immune to it. Strength was measured by resistance, and vulnerability was equated with weakness.

But beneath these cultural myths lies a quiet distortion, one that has cost humanity dearly. In trying to appear fearless, we have become emotionally blind. In attempting to conquer fear, we have declared war on our own intelligence.

Fear, as we have come to understand through our journey in this book, is not an error in human design. It is a form of sensitivity, the body's wisdom speaking in its ancient language. The one who feels deeply is not weak; he is alive. Yet society, in its race for efficiency, control, and image, has taught people to numb this sensitivity. We armor the heart, suppress tears, hide our trembling hands, and smile when every cell inside is quivering. We call this "strength." But it is not strength, it is strain.

A mind that constantly suppresses its natural signals cannot be at peace. Fear that is silenced does not disappear; it migrates. It hides in tension, insomnia, irritation, overwork, or emotional fatigue. It begins to leak into our relationships and ambitions, disguised as control, jealousy, or perfectionism. We become so busy maintaining the mask of confidence that we forget the essence of confidence, awareness of one's own humanity.

True fearlessness does not emerge from denial; it emerges from dialogue. It begins when we sit quietly with our fears, not to judge them, but to listen. When you ask, "What are you trying to tell me?" you initiate the first act of courage. Most people think courage is the opposite of fear. It is not. Courage is intimacy with fear. It is the willingness to be honest, to say, Yes, I am afraid. But I am here, and I will stay with this feeling until I understand it.

That simple act changes everything. Fear no longer remains a monster lurking in the dark corners of the mind; it becomes a messenger carrying truth. It tells you what matters most to you, your family, your freedom, your identity, your peace. Fear points toward your values. It shows you where you are still attached, where you still identify with what can be lost. If you listen long enough, fear becomes a map of love, every fear traces back to something you deeply care about. The fear of failure hides the desire to grow. The fear of rejection conceals the longing to belong. The fear of death reveals the yearning to live fully before the end.

When seen in this light, fearlessness is not about having no fear; it is about having no conflict with fear. The fearless person still feels fear, but without shame, without panic, without resistance. They meet fear as a wise friend who arrives uninvited but always with purpose. They have learned the language of energy rather than the language of war.

The misunderstanding of fearlessness often begins early in life. Children are told, "Don't be scared," as though fear were an error rather than a natural emotion. We teach them to hide vulnerability before we teach them how to understand it. We glorify strength as silence and mistake emotional maturity for emotional suppression. By the time they become adults, most people have learned to mistrust their own feelings. They have become strangers to themselves, polished on the outside, restless within.

And yet, deep down, every soul longs for permission, permission to be honest, fragile, uncertain, human. The irony is that this permission, once given, does not make a person weaker; it makes them infinitely stronger. Because when you stop pretending to be fearless, you stop wasting energy on maintaining the illusion. That energy, once freed, becomes awareness. Awareness becomes peace. And peace is the highest form of strength.

If you observe those who truly live fearlessly, not the loud ones, but the luminous ones, you will notice something striking. They do not try to control life; they cooperate with it. They do not demand certainty; they rest in trust. They speak truthfully but without aggression, act decisively but without arrogance, and face loss without despair. Their calmness is not learned from books; it is born from deep reconciliation with life's rhythm. They have stopped asking for life to be predictable and have begun participating in its mystery.

There is a quiet confidence that comes from this reconciliation, a confidence that does not shout but smiles. It is not the confidence of "I can handle anything," but the confidence of "Whatever comes, I will learn." This subtle shift marks the difference between the fearful achiever and the fearless human. The achiever demands control; the fearless person practices surrender. The achiever wants certainty before acting; the fearless one acts in the presence of uncertainty.

True fearlessness is not a performance of strength; it is a presence of sincerity. It does not seek to impress; it seeks to understand. It is less about domination and more about connection, connection with yourself, with others, and with the larger intelligence that governs all of existence.

Fearless living, then, begins with humility. The humble are not afraid because they do not demand life to obey their plans. They flow with it. They are curious instead of cautious, responsive instead of reactive. Their strength is quiet because it is rooted in trust. They know that life is not against them, it is guiding them, teaching them, sometimes gently, sometimes fiercely, but always toward awakening.

When we realize this, the old image of fearlessness collapses, the one built on bravado and denial. In its place emerges a new vision- the soft, radiant strength of someone fully present, fully human. A person who can cry without guilt, laugh without reason, rest without worry, and act without fear of outcome. That is the art of true fearlessness, not the hard edge of control, but the open palm of acceptance.

To live fearlessly is to be willing to meet life exactly as it is, unpredictable, uncontrollable, yet exquisitely intelligent. It is to say "yes" to existence in all its colors, without editing, without retreat. The fearless life is not a destination you reach once fear disappears; it is the posture of awareness in motion, walking hand in hand with fear, smiling, listening, and learning, until fear itself becomes love in another form.

The Three Dimensions of Fearless Living-

Fearlessness is not a single act of courage. It is a state of coherence, a harmony between mind, heart, and life. It emerges when awareness sharpens, trust deepens, and action flows without fear of outcome. These are not steps to climb but dimensions to awaken. Together, they form the art of living fearlessly.

Awareness, Seeing Fear as a Signal, Not a Verdict-

Every feeling begins as a whisper. Fear does not enter like an enemy; it rises like a messenger. It comes quietly, long before the body trembles or the mind spirals. A tightening in the breath, a quickening pulse, a subtle unease, these are not punishments but signals. They tell us that attention is required, that something precious needs care.

Yet most people react to these signals with resistance. The mind rushes to label- Something is wrong. I must escape. That very reaction magnifies fear. The signal becomes static; the whisper turns into noise. But when awareness enters, everything changes. Awareness does not fight fear; it observes it. It does not amplify sensation with stories; it meets sensation with silence. It watches without judgment, and in that stillness, the body begins to settle, the breath lengthens, and clarity emerges.

Awareness is the first act of courage because it interrupts the reflex of flight. It is the decision to stay, to remain present with what feels uncomfortable until its nature reveals itself. You begin to see that fear is not absolute; it fluctuates. It rises, peaks, and fades. No emotion sustains itself forever. By simply observing, you discover something astonishing- you are not the fear. You are the awareness witnessing it. The storm no longer defines the sky.

This shift from identification to observation is the foundation of fearless living. You stop asking, How do I get rid of fear? and start asking, What is fear showing me? In that question, fear turns from adversary to ally. Awareness turns pain into perspective.

Trust, Realizing You Are Supported by Life's Intelligence-

If awareness shows that fear is not the enemy, trust reveals that life is not either. Trust is not belief; belief is fragile and depends on proof. Trust is deeper, it is the quiet confidence that the same intelligence that spins galaxies also guides your small steps. It is the recognition that life, in its vast orchestration, rarely makes mistakes.

Fear thrives in separation, the feeling that you are alone, isolated, and must control everything. Trust dissolves that illusion. When you begin to see how seamlessly life functions, how your heartbeat, digestion, and sleep happen without your command, you realize that you are not the manager of existence, only its participant. Something larger is already holding everything together.

Trust begins in small acts. You trust the morning to arrive after night. You trust the ground to hold your weight. You trust the seed to sprout when it is ready. Then you extend that same trust inward- perhaps my path too is unfolding in its right rhythm. This shift doesn't erase difficulty, but it removes despair. You stop wrestling with "why," and begin resting in "what is."

People often misunderstand trust as passivity, but trust is participation without panic. It allows action without agitation. When you trust, you act not because you fear failure but because you love to express. You stop performing for outcomes and start participating in creation. Your work becomes prayer; your effort becomes gratitude.

When trust matures, even uncertainty becomes sacred. You realize that not knowing is the condition for discovery. The future no longer frightens you; it invites you. Life becomes less about security and more about connection, connection to the intelligence that breathes through everything. This connection is what makes the fearless heart so serene- it has surrendered the burden of control and chosen the adventure of trust.

Engagement, Acting Despite Uncertainty-

Awareness gives clarity; trust gives grounding; engagement gives motion. Fearlessness cannot remain philosophical, it must find expression in action. Without engagement, awareness becomes reflection, and trust becomes comfort. Engagement is how understanding becomes embodiment.

To engage with life fearlessly does not mean reckless bravery. It means moving forward even when the outcome is unknown, not because you are sure of success, but because you are sure of your intention. It is the quiet, daily choice to keep living, loving, creating, and learning in a world that guarantees neither permanence nor perfection.

Every act of engagement, whether it is speaking truth, beginning a project, forgiving someone, or simply showing up, is a declaration- I choose participation over paralysis. This is the real meaning of courage, not absence of fear, but refusal to obey it.

Fearless engagement has a rhythm. It moves between action and stillness, doing and pausing, expression and reflection. Just as music depends on silence, courageous living depends on rest. When you rest consciously, you allow wisdom to settle into your actions. Fearless people are not constantly busy; they are deeply deliberate. Every gesture is infused with awareness.

Engagement also means embracing imperfection. You learn that no step forward is ever wasted, even the missteps. Mistakes are not failures; they are refinements. Every fear faced expands your capacity for life. Each time you move through discomfort instead of around it, you reclaim energy that was once trapped in avoidance. That reclaimed energy becomes creativity, the joy of participating in life's unfolding.

Ultimately, engagement completes the cycle of fearless living. Awareness gives insight, trust gives faith, and engagement gives embodiment. When all three align, life becomes both spontaneous and stable. You no longer chase meaning; you live it. You no longer search for peace; you express it. You realize that fearlessness is not a condition you reach but a rhythm you maintain, a dance between knowing, trusting, and doing.

Fearlessness is therefore not a single moment of victory; it is a lifelong dialogue between consciousness and creation. Each day, awareness listens, trust steadies, and engagement moves. The mind that once lived in resistance now lives in rhythm. And in that rhythm, there is not the silence of emptiness, but the silence of completeness, the soundless music of a life lived fully awake.

Fearless Communication-

Fear enters communication more often than we realize. It hides behind politeness, pride, or anger. We speak to impress, defend, or control, rarely to express. Much of what we call "conversation" is a subtle exchange of fear, the fear of being judged, misunderstood, or dismissed. When fear takes hold, communication loses its purpose. Words become weapons or shields instead of instruments of understanding.

To communicate fearlessly, we must first understand the nature of speech itself. Speech is not simply the act of using words; it is the translation of thought into vibration. When thought is disturbed by insecurity, words carry that disturbance forward. That is why some conversations, even when polite, leave behind a sense of exhaustion, they are filled with unspoken tension.

Fearless communication begins with clarity of intention. It is not about proving who is right; it is about seeking what is true. The moment you stop trying to defend your image and begin focusing on understanding, your tone changes, your words simplify, and your presence strengthens. People can feel when you speak from authenticity rather than anxiety. Truth has its own quiet confidence.

To speak truthfully is not the same as to speak harshly. Many people confuse bluntness with honesty and aggression with strength. But truth does not need force; it needs precision. Words spoken in awareness cut deeper than words shouted in anger. Fearless speech is calm speech, rooted, measured, and unpretentious. It respects the dignity of the listener, even when delivering uncomfortable truths.

This kind of communication requires emotional maturity. You must learn to pause before you speak, to examine the motive behind your words. Ask yourself- Am I saying this to be understood or to be superior? Am I trying to express or to escape? These questions reveal the hidden fears that shape our language. The act of pausing is not hesitation; it is intelligence. In that short moment of awareness, words are refined into truth.

Fearless communication also includes the ability to admit uncertainty. There is immense power in saying, "I don't know." Such honesty disarms conflict because it removes the ego's armor. When you stop pretending to know everything, you create space for genuine dialogue. Humility becomes the bridge where understanding meets understanding.

Equally important is the courage to listen. Most people listen only to reply, not to understand. Fearless listening means allowing another person's truth to exist without immediately measuring it against your own. You listen not as an opponent preparing a response, but as a witness allowing meaning to unfold. When you listen like this, even disagreement feels safe, because both participants feel seen rather than threatened.

Conflict loses its sharpness when awareness enters. The goal is no longer victory but clarity. You can stand by your view without aggression because you no longer need to be right, you simply need to be real. When authenticity becomes the aim, truth naturally emerges between people, often without debate. The mind that listens fearlessly discovers that communication is not a battle but a bridge.

This kind of communication does not come from self-control; it comes from self-awareness. You cannot speak peacefully if your mind is in turmoil. You cannot listen deeply if you are internally defensive. The tone of your voice always reveals the tone of your mind. That is why cultivating inner stillness is essential. When your mind is quiet, your words become clear, and your presence alone communicates more than language ever could.

In relationships, personal or professional, fearless communication transforms everything. When people know that your words are honest but kind, they begin to trust your silence too. When they sense that you speak not from fear but from awareness, they stop guarding themselves. Communication becomes cooperation. Even disagreement becomes a form of mutual growth.

Fearless speech, then, is not a skill to master; it is the natural outcome of a calm mind. The more you understand yourself, the more you understand how to speak. The less you try to impress, the more your presence impresses. When the mind is free from the need to dominate or to hide, it begins to express truth without distortion.

In such speech there is no aggression, no flattery, and no manipulation, only clarity. And from clarity arises peace, because where there is nothing to hide, there is nothing to fear.

Fearless attention-

Fear often disguises itself as ambition. It hides behind phrases like "I need to stay relevant," "I can't afford to fail," or "I must be the best." At first glance, these thoughts seem positive, signs of a motivated, driven person. But beneath them lies an unspoken anxiety- the fear of being left behind, the fear of not being enough, the fear that one's worth depends on performance.

Work becomes a stage for this fear to perform endlessly. We wake up with it, carry it into meetings, and measure our value by the approval it earns. Instead of being an expression of life's intelligence, work turns into a competition for survival. The creative spark that once felt like joy is slowly replaced by the pressure to keep proving.

But real work, the kind that nourishes both the doer and the world, cannot grow in fear. It flourishes only in freedom.

Fearless work does not begin with skill; it begins with clarity of purpose. When you understand why you are working, not just what you are working for, your relationship with effort changes completely. You stop working to prove, and start working to express. You no longer chase recognition; you chase refinement. What others call success becomes a by-product, not the goal.

The truth is, competition is rarely about others, it is a conflict within the self. We compete with imagined versions of who we should be, rather than evolve from who we truly are.

Fearless individuals understand this distinction deeply. They are not indifferent to achievement, but they approach it differently. Their focus is creation, not comparison. They work from fullness, not fear.

When the mind is free from the obsession of "doing better than," it begins to see possibilities instead of threats. Collaboration replaces rivalry. Learning becomes continuous because mistakes are no longer punishable, they are simply steps in the unfolding of mastery. This shift in attitude transforms not just results, but the entire experience of work itself.

Fearless work is not lazy; it is purposeful. It demands full engagement, but never tension. It is intense, but not anxious. It is disciplined, but not rigid. In such a state, productivity is no longer about the number of hours but the depth of presence within them. A single hour of clear focus can often accomplish what ten anxious hours cannot.

To work without fear is to trust the intelligence of the process. There are moments when ideas dry up, when nothing seems to move forward. The fearful mind interprets these pauses as failure. But the fearless mind sees them as part of creation's rhythm, moments of gathering, integration, or invisible growth. Just as night prepares the soil for dawn, silence prepares the mind for insight.

This is why rest is not the opposite of work; it is part of it. The most profound creativity arises when you stop forcing the outcome and allow inspiration to flow naturally. Pressure fragments awareness; patience unites it. The world teaches us to "hustle harder," but the universe often rewards those who know when to pause.

Fearless work also requires emotional honesty. Many people burn out not from overwork but from working against their own truth. They stay in roles that no longer resonate, follow paths that feel disconnected, or suppress ideas that their environment doesn't yet understand. Over time, this inner resistance drains vitality.

To work fearlessly is to align your actions with your values, even when it costs comfort. It means having the courage to say, "This is not my path," and the humility to begin again.

The fearless worker is not driven by external validation; they are guided by inner alignment. Their confidence is not arrogance, it is calm assurance born from authenticity. They do not measure their worth by titles, but by the honesty of their effort. They understand that real success is not about reaching higher positions, but deeper states of peace.

And when fear does appear, as it will, they meet it as a signal, not an obstacle. Fear becomes information, revealing where attachment hides or where clarity is missing. Once seen, it dissolves, and energy flows freely again. In this way, work becomes not just a means of earning, but a form of awakening, a practice that refines awareness through action.

Imagine a world where every person worked not out of fear of losing, but out of love for contributing. Where competition evolved into collaboration, and innovation was born from curiosity rather than comparison. In that world, work would no longer be a burden; it would be worship, not in the religious sense, but as an act of harmony between human intelligence and the universal order.

Fearless work is, in the end, not about what you do but how you do it. When your mind is steady, your hands move differently. When your heart is calm, your ideas mature naturally. The task, no matter how ordinary, becomes meaningful because it carries the fragrance of presence. Every email, every design, every effort, every pause becomes a quiet affirmation of trust, that life is not against you, it is working with you, through you.

And once you understand this, work is no longer a race.
It becomes a rhythm, steady, alive, and deeply fulfilling.

Fearless Relationships-

Love and fear often live close together. We fear losing those we love, fear not being loved enough, fear change, distance, or silence. At first, these fears look like care. We hold tighter, speak softer, promise more, and build invisible walls around what we cherish. But love that is wrapped in fear slowly forgets how to breathe. What begins as devotion can quietly turn into dependence, and what begins as protection becomes control.

To love fearlessly is to unlearn this habit of holding. It is to understand that connection and possession are not the same. Connection grows in freedom; possession suffocates it. Love that depends on ownership is not love, it is anxiety pretending to care.

Fearless love begins when we realize that love is not something to be earned or secured; it is something that flows naturally when we are complete within ourselves. When a heart is full, it does not beg, it overflows. It gives because giving is its nature. It does not cling to receive comfort; it radiates warmth because that is what it is made of. Such love says, "I love you because I am whole," not "I love you because I need."

The fearful mind confuses attachment with affection. It measures love in gestures and attention, as if silence or space means loss. But life is made of change, and every soul must move according to its own rhythm. When we love with awareness, we trust this rhythm. We allow others to grow, to shift, to explore, even to drift away for a while, because what is real does not disappear in distance. True love does not weaken when it is unspoken; it deepens in understanding.

Fearless love speaks plainly, not to win or defend but to connect. It listens quietly, not to reply but to feel. It does not manipulate emotion to gain security. It does not hide behind politeness to avoid truth. It trusts that honesty, even when uncomfortable, is the highest form of respect. In fearless relationships, words become lighter, and silence becomes safe. There is no need to prove, perform, or protect an image of togetherness. There is only presence, two beings meeting as they are, without masks, without demand.

To love fearlessly is also to know when to let go. Compassion does not require captivity. Awareness teaches that sometimes the most loving act is to release what no longer nurtures the soul. When affection turns into burden, when togetherness begins to wound, love's wisdom whispers that staying may harm more than parting. Fearless love walks away without bitterness because it sees that endings, too, belong to the order of life. It thanks what was shared, blesses what was learned, and allows what must change to change.

Such love understands that pain is not proof of failure. It is simply the cost of deep connection, the reminder that what touched you mattered. Fearless love turns even separation into gratitude, transforming memories into quiet teachers rather than sharp regrets.

When fear leaves love, trust takes its place. Trust does not ask for guarantees. It does not demand constant reassurance. It believes that what is real will remain, and what is not will fade as it must. This trust frees both people to live truthfully, to express rather than impress, to give without keeping score. In this freedom, love matures. It becomes less about how long it lasts and more about how deeply it is lived.

Love without possession is not detached or indifferent; it is warm, steady, and alive. It honors individuality and celebrates togetherness without confusion. It lets two journeys run parallel, not fused, not forced, moving in harmony rather than control. In such love, there is no fear of tomorrow, because every moment is already complete.

To love in this way is to see relationships not as anchors, but as mirrors, each person reflecting the beauty and the shadows that already exist within us. Every meeting, every heartbreak, every silence reveals something about who we are, what we fear, and how much we can grow.

Fearless love is the natural state of a heart that remembers its source. It is love that flows like breath, effortless, giving, receiving, releasing. It trusts the divine intelligence that connects souls for reasons beyond comprehension. And because it trusts, it never clings.

When love becomes fearless, it stops asking, "Will this last?" and begins asking, "Am I fully present now?" That question turns every relationship into a sacred space, alive, conscious, and free from the shadow of possession.

Fearless Solitude-

Modern life teaches us many things, how to speak, connect, compete, and collaborate, but it rarely teaches us how to be alone. We are raised to believe that solitude is a sign of emptiness, that silence means something is missing, and that stillness is wasted time. We fill every gap in our day with motion, screens, music, voices, tasks, as if quiet itself were an enemy. Yet, beneath all the noise we keep alive, something inside us longs for pause. It waits, patiently, for the moment when we finally turn inward and listen.

Silence frightens people because in silence, the unspoken begins to speak. The mind, deprived of distraction, starts revealing its stored memories and unprocessed feelings. Every regret, every desire, every fear that was drowned in noise begins to surface. It is not the silence we fear, it is the encounter with ourselves.

But solitude, when embraced consciously, becomes the purest form of companionship. To be fearlessly alone is not to reject the world but to rediscover your own company. It is to sit quietly and meet your presence without escape, to watch the mind's parade of thoughts without chasing or judging them. At first, it feels uncomfortable, like standing under a light that reveals too much. Then, slowly, the restlessness settles. The mind, realizing that it is being observed, begins to soften. What once felt like emptiness begins to feel like space.

When you stay long enough in that space, you start to see the architecture of your inner world. Thoughts rise and fall like tides, emotions pass like clouds, and underneath it all, you notice something constant, an awareness untouched by any of it. You realize that loneliness was never the absence of others; it was the unfamiliarity with your own presence.

In solitude, masks fall away. The face you wear for approval dissolves. You stop performing kindness or strength to be accepted. You begin to experience yourself without roles, without comparisons, without narrative. It is startling at first, and then, deeply peaceful. For the first time, you are not trying to be anyone. You are simply being.

In that stillness, subtle rhythms emerge, the sound of your own breath, the hum of existence, the quiet pulse of life moving through you. You begin to hear the voice beneath thought, not the mind's chatter, but the deeper knowing that whispers between thoughts. From that silence, clarity is born. You begin to see what truly matters, what you truly want, and what you can release. Decisions that once felt impossible begin to feel simple. The noise of the world fades, and what remains is pure intelligence, not learned, but remembered.

Fearless solitude is not withdrawal; it is renewal. The world teaches us to run endlessly outward, but solitude invites us back home. It is the cleansing of the senses, the resetting of rhythm, the realignment of mind and heart. In that aloneness, you gather back the energy scattered in a thousand directions. You return to your own center, and from that center, life begins again.

To be alone and at ease is a rare strength. Most people can only meet others through need, needing approval, needing attention, needing distraction. But one who can sit joyfully in their own presence meets the world differently. They approach others not to take, but to share. Their relationships stop being a remedy for emptiness and become an extension of fullness. They no longer cling; they connect. They no longer demand; they give.

Fearless solitude teaches completeness, and completeness births unconditional love. For when you have met yourself fully, you no longer fear abandonment, you cannot be abandoned by the world when you have discovered your own company. You no longer chase affection as validation; love flows naturally through you as part of being alive. And when you return to the world after such solitude, you bring clarity instead of confusion, calm instead of urgency, compassion instead of need.

Solitude is not a punishment from life; it is an invitation from life to meet its most profound truth, that everything you have been searching for already resides within you. Every time you sit alone in silence and do nothing but breathe, you are not wasting time; you are listening to eternity speaking softly through your own heart.

Fearless solitude is the gateway to peace. It does not isolate you from life; it reunites you with it. In silence, you meet the divine rhythm that animates all things, the quiet intelligence that breathes through your breath and beats through your heart. Once you touch that presence, you understand- you were never truly alone. You were simply surrounded by a presence too vast to be seen, waiting for you to notice.

Fearless Change-

Every change carries a small death, the death of habit, identity, and certainty. Even positive changes can feel uncomfortable because they dissolve the familiar ground beneath us. The mind, shaped by repetition, confuses stability with safety. It believes that if things remain the same, it can rest. But life was never designed for sameness. It is a continuous motion, a current that flows through every form, constantly creating, dissolving, and recreating.

To resist change is to resist life itself. Yet most suffering begins in that resistance. The mind clings to what it knows, even when what it knows has become too small. It chooses familiarity over freedom because uncertainty feels like danger. But real danger lies in stagnation. What does not move, decays. What refuses to evolve, eventually breaks.

Fearless living does not mean predicting or controlling change; it means learning to move with it, to partner with the intelligence that guides evolution. When you stop asking, "Why is this happening to me?" and start asking, "What is this teaching me?" the entire quality of experience transforms. Endings stop feeling like punishment; they start revealing purpose.

Every ending in life, a job, a phase, a relationship, even an old version of yourself, carries within it a silent promise- the promise of renewal. What feels like loss is often life clearing space for something higher to unfold. When fear arises, it is only because the mind cannot yet see the design behind the dismantling. The unseen feels like chaos, but change is not chaos; it is choreography unseen.

Look at nature- no season resists another. The trees do not panic when winter comes; they shed what they no longer need and rest. The sky does not mourn the setting sun; it trusts that dawn will return. The river does not weep when it meets the ocean; it fulfills its purpose. Every part of creation understands the rhythm of change. Only the human mind tries to stop the music.

Fearless change begins when you breathe through uncertainty instead of fighting it.

When discomfort appears, you remind yourself, "This too is life moving." You stop treating fear as a warning and begin seeing it as an invitation, an opportunity to expand your capacity for the unknown. Growth always feels unfamiliar because it demands you to step beyond what you have already mastered. It is the feeling of your own consciousness stretching into new territory.

Adaptability becomes your real strength. It is not about passivity or surrendering your will; it is about flexibility, the ability to bend without breaking, to pause without freezing, to reinvent without regret. The mind that trusts change is not weak; it is wise. It knows that no situation is permanent, and therefore nothing is ever truly lost. Life replaces what it removes, multiplies what it tests, and transforms what it challenges.

To adapt fearlessly is to see that uncertainty is not a void but a bridge, a passage between what was and what is becoming. The only reason the bridge feels shaky is because you are still in motion. Once you arrive, it will make sense. The pain you feel during transition is not the end of the story; it is the discomfort of unfolding wings.

When you begin to live this way, change stops being something to survive and becomes something to collaborate with. You no longer pray for the old to return; you learn to bless the new that is forming. You stop calling endings "loss" and start calling them "graduations." You realize that the future is not a threat but an open field waiting for your participation.

And one day, as you look back, you will see that every unexpected turn, every departure, detour, and delay, was not random. It was the choreography of a greater intelligence gently shaping your path toward what you were meant to become.

Fearless change is not the absence of uncertainty; it is the confidence that whatever comes, you will meet it fully. Because you have already learned, through solitude, through surrender, through silence, that what you truly are does not change. The world around you moves endlessly, but the awareness within you remains still, steady, eternal.

When you discover that still point, change no longer threatens you.
It becomes your rhythm, your teacher, your companion.
And then, even uncertainty feels like home.

12 THE FLOW OF THOUGHTS

There are moments when the mind feels like a storm, every gust a thought, every drop a memory. It moves unpredictably, sometimes gently, sometimes with force, yet if you pause and truly observe, you realize something remarkable- the storm was never against you. It was simply the sky moving through its own rhythm.

Thoughts, too, are like that, movements of consciousness passing across the vast expanse of awareness. They are not personal, even though we spend most of our lives believing they are. They arise from impressions gathered through time, things we've seen, heard, imagined, or remembered, and dissolve back into the same silence from which they came. Each thought, no matter how loud or heavy, is temporary. It comes to express, to release, and to move on.

Yet the human mind, caught in its habit of control, mistakes movement for meaning. We start believing that our thoughts define us, that every passing idea is a reflection of who we are. A single negative thought, if left alone, would fade like morning mist under sunlight. But when we engage with it, when we resist, analyze, or fear it, we feed it energy. Just as fire grows with the wind, a thought expands with attention.

In truth, the mind was never meant to be a battlefield. It was designed as a river, a continuous flow of impressions, memories, sensations, and possibilities. Its purpose is not to stay still but to move, to process, to create. The flow itself is natural and necessary. Without thought, there is no imagination, no reflection, no discovery. But problems arise when we stop flowing with it and begin identifying with every wave.

We say, "I am anxious," forgetting that anxiety is simply a wave passing through. We say, "I am broken," forgetting that the feeling of brokenness is only a current in motion. The ocean is never defined by its waves; it is defined by its depth. And we, too, are not defined by our thoughts but by the awareness in which those thoughts appear and disappear.

The art of living fearlessly begins with this realization, that you are not your thoughts, you are the space that holds them. Thoughts rise, move, dissolve, and rise again, but the sky of awareness remains untouched. The mind changes its weather, but consciousness never loses its calm.

To live in the flow of thoughts is not to silence the mind; it is to stop fighting with it. When a thought appears, you allow it. You watch it arrive, stay, and leave. You don't rush to judge, react, or fix it. You recognize it as part of life's rhythm, one more movement in the grand dance of existence.

Some thoughts bring peace, others bring discomfort. Both are part of the same intelligence trying to communicate through you. Some are echoes of the past; others are glimpses of possibility. But none are permanent, and none can imprison you once you stop feeding them with fear.

Just as the river carries fallen leaves without resistance, your awareness can carry every thought effortlessly when you stop grasping at them. Let them pass. Let them flow. And as they move, you will begin to sense something profound, that behind every thought, beneath every emotion, there exists a silence that is never disturbed. That silence is not emptiness; it is your essence.

To reach it, you don't need to think more clearly, you need to think less personally.

You don't need to escape your thoughts, you need to understand their nature. And once you do, you realize that even your most fearful thoughts were never enemies; they were simply unrecognized movements of life, asking for your attention and forgiveness before returning to peace.

This is the flow of thoughts, the ever-moving, ever-renewing current that, when understood, no longer threatens you. It becomes your teacher, your companion, and eventually, your reflection.

For the one who learns to watch the mind without resistance, life itself becomes meditation.

A River That Never Stops Flowing-

Imagine a river flowing past you, its water moving endlessly, sometimes calm, sometimes restless. You cannot stop the river; that is its nature. But you can choose how you meet it. You can sit by its bank and watch the current move with quiet wonder, or you can dive in without awareness and be swept away by its force.

The mind is that river. Thoughts, pleasant or painful, bright or heavy, are its waves. They rise, carry the stories of your life, and dissolve back into the flow. When you identify too much with them, you lose your footing. You get caught in their current, pulled along by memories, fears, or desires that were never meant to define you. But when you observe them from the stillness of awareness, you begin to see differently. You realize that the river was never your enemy. It was only life in motion, intelligence unfolding in its own rhythm.

The wise do not fight their thoughts; they flow with them, untouched. They know that movement is the nature of the mind, and stillness is the nature of awareness. They understand that even turbulent waters eventually find calm when not disturbed. The river does not need to stop for you to find peace; you only need to stop mistaking yourself for the river.

The Fragility of Negative Thoughts-

Compared to truth, illusion is fragile. Compared to clarity, confusion is short-lived. Negative thoughts seem powerful, but only because they shout. They rise suddenly, filling the mind with noise and urgency, as though demanding attention. Yet, their strength is borrowed; they exist only for as long as we keep listening.

A thought by itself is nothing more than a small movement of energy, a flicker in the vast current of consciousness. Left alone, it disappears as quietly as it came. But the moment we react, the moment we analyze, resist, or fear it, we breathe life into it. Just as fire grows with wind, a thought expands with attention.

A single passing doubt, when replayed and examined repeatedly, becomes a story. The mind begins to imagine, to dramatize, to build layers of meaning around it. "What if" becomes "probably," and "probably" soon feels like "truth." The original thought might have been brief and harmless, but our involvement turns it into a storm.

And yet, no storm lasts forever. Darkness has no life of its own; it only appears where light is absent. In the same way, negative thoughts cannot survive under the steady light of awareness. The moment we see them clearly, not suppress, not deny, just see, they begin to fade. Awareness does not fight thoughts; it transforms them simply by shining upon them.

This is why wisdom has always taught the power of observation. When a thought arises, you do not need to chase it away or argue with it. You simply watch it come, stay, and go. Just as the ocean allows its waves, you allow the mind to move without identifying with every motion.

Every negative thought carries information. It is not a curse, but a signal. Fear tells you where you have forgotten your courage. Jealousy shows you where gratitude is missing. Anger reveals where pain has been left unattended. When you see them this way, even the darkest thoughts begin to serve you. They stop being threats and become teachers.

The trouble begins only when we fight them. The moment you resist, the thought resists back. It grows louder, heavier, more convincing. But once you meet it with understanding, once you acknowledge it and stop arguing, it loses its foundation. Like smoke rising into open air, it disperses naturally.

The sky is never harmed by clouds. Storms pass, but the sky remains untouched. In the same way, your consciousness remains pure and complete no matter how many thoughts pass through it. Even when fear feels overwhelming, the one who observes that fear is always calm. You may forget this truth, but it never stops being true.

Negative thoughts are fragile because they depend entirely on your participation. They cannot sustain themselves. They need you to feed them attention, to repeat their story, to believe their message. The moment you withdraw that energy, they collapse. They return to the silence from which they came.

And in that silence, you realize something remarkable- you were never at war with your own mind. The storm was never against you. It was only energy asking to be recognized, emotion seeking its place, thought returning home.

Living fearlessly does not mean eliminating negative thoughts. It means seeing them for what they are, transient, powerless, and temporary. You no longer tremble when they appear because you know they cannot stay. You no longer chase them away because you know they cannot harm you.

The sky does not fear the storm because it knows its own vastness. Likewise, awareness does not fear the mind because it knows that all thoughts, no matter how dark, arise and dissolve within it. When you remember this, fear loses its grip. You stop running, you stop resisting, and slowly, you start smiling at the passing clouds of thought, because you finally understand- they were never the problem. Forgetting your own sky was.

The Law of Duality and Divine Design-

If we pause long enough to look carefully at the world around us, we find that every aspect of existence speaks in pairs. Day and night, life and death, joy and sorrow, creation and destruction, all stand as two sides of a single pulse. This rhythm of opposites is not chaos; it is harmony expressed in contrast. The universe sustains itself through balance, not uniformity.

In this vast design, duality is not a mistake to be solved but a law to be understood. Every emotion, thought, or event holds its complement within it. Happiness carries the memory of sadness; certainty leans against the shadow of doubt. The existence of one makes the experience of the other possible. Without darkness, there would be no awareness of light. Without pain, love would not feel precious.

When people suffer, they often ask why negative emotions exist, why fear, grief, or loss are allowed to touch a life that longs for peace. But to remove pain from creation would be to remove depth from the human heart. The divine design allows opposites so that understanding may unfold through experience. Fear teaches courage, doubt sharpens faith, and impermanence makes every moment sacred.

The great misunderstanding arises when we try to cling to one side and reject the other. We want joy without sorrow, growth without struggle, love without loss. Yet this craving breaks the very balance that sustains harmony. The refusal to accept life's full spectrum is what gives birth to inner conflict. We begin to resist what was never meant to be resisted, the natural ebb and flow of existence.

In this design, negative thoughts and emotions are not punishments; they are participants. They exist to guide awareness back to its center. The same energy that frightens us can awaken us, if we meet it without resistance. When the mind stops labeling one half as "good" and the other as "bad," both are seen as movement, waves of one ocean.

The divine design does not promise comfort; it promises completeness. It offers every experience required for a being to grow toward awareness. What we call suffering is often the friction of transformation, the breaking of an old shell that no longer fits the soul within.

When we begin to live with this understanding, fear softens. Pain becomes less of an enemy and more of a signal. Even doubt starts to feel sacred because it means life is asking us to look deeper. Duality is not a test of endurance; it is a mirror that shows us both the shadow and the light within ourselves.

To live wisely is to move with both, to smile in joy and remain open in sorrow, to walk through uncertainty with curiosity rather than control. The universe does not demand that we eliminate contrast; it invites us to recognize its purpose. The pulse of opposites keeps the cosmos alive. When we stop fighting that pulse, we begin to live in rhythm with creation itself.

The Three Practices of Flow-

Every river needs movement, and every movement needs rhythm. The human mind, too, is a river, an endless stream of thoughts, sensations, and feelings flowing through the landscape of awareness. To live peacefully within it, we must learn how to move with its current rather than drown in it. The flow of life cannot be controlled, but it can be understood. And that understanding rests on three timeless practices- Observation, Surrender, and Celebration.

Observation-

The first step toward freedom from mental turbulence is the simplest and yet the hardest, to observe. Observation means watching the mind without judgment, as though it were a sky where clouds come and go. When a thought appears, you do not name it, label it, or fight it. You simply notice it.

This practice is powerful because it breaks identification. The moment you observe, you create distance between the thought and the thinker. That distance is awareness. And awareness, by its very nature, dissolves confusion.

A negative thought can only harm you when you believe it is "yours." Once you see it as a movement of energy passing through, its grip weakens. It may still pass, but it no longer drags you with it. The storm moves, but you remain still.

Observation is not detachment, it is intimacy without entanglement. You begin to understand the pattern of your own mind- how fear arises, how it feeds on imagination, how it fades when ignored. Over time, you realize that the mind was never the enemy; misunderstanding was. You stop fighting, and in that quiet, you begin to see truth.

Surrender-

Observation brings clarity, but clarity alone does not dissolve resistance. To truly flow with life, one must surrender.

Surrender does not mean defeat or passivity. It is the intelligent act of recognizing what lies beyond your control. When you surrender, you stop trying to push the river in a direction of your choosing. You allow it to carry you, trusting that its current knows the destination better than you do.

We often mistake control for strength, but in truth, control is fear disguised as responsibility. The mind believes that if it stops holding on, everything will collapse. Yet when you let go, you discover something miraculous, the world continues to function, and often, far more beautifully than when you interfered.

Surrender brings relief because it restores the natural order. It teaches that life is self-balancing. Every rise has a fall, and every fall prepares another rise. When you stop resisting, you begin to participate in this divine rhythm rather than struggle against it.

In surrender, even pain becomes purposeful. You start to see that what once felt like punishment was actually preparation. What looked like loss was space being cleared for renewal. The mind relaxes, the heart opens, and the burden of constant control finally lifts.

Celebration-

Understanding opens the eyes, surrender opens the heart, but celebration, celebration opens the soul. It is the flowering of acceptance, the moment when a person no longer resists the flow of life but begins to dance with it.

To celebrate is to say *yes* to existence, not selectively, not only when it brings comfort or success, but even when it challenges, humbles, or unsettles. It is to look at both joy and sorrow and bow to them with equal reverence. For one who has truly seen the rhythm of life, there is no longer "good" and "bad." There is only movement, and every movement has meaning.

Celebration is not about perfection. It is not the denial of pain or the exaggeration of pleasure. It is the quiet recognition that life, in all its unpredictability, is sacred. To celebrate means to participate consciously, to stand in the middle of chaos and still remember that existence itself is a gift. You dance not because life has gone your way, but because you are here, awake, breathing, capable of seeing, feeling, and being.

When you begin to celebrate, every act becomes prayer. Walking, speaking, eating, resting, all transform into moments of reverence. You laugh not because everything is pleasant, but because fear has lost its hold on you. You realize that laughter is not the absence of pain but the presence of understanding.

In celebration, emotions reveal their divine purpose. Happiness deepens into gratitude; sadness becomes compassion. Fear softens into humility, and uncertainty opens into curiosity. The same energy that once caused anxiety begins to move through you as creativity and insight. What was once heaviness now feels like rhythm.

To celebrate does not mean to indulge or to escape. It means to see life as it is, raw, mysterious, imperfect, and still to whisper "thank you." It is an act of alignment with the larger intelligence that governs this universe, a surrender to the wisdom that orchestrates even the moments we do not understand.

When you celebrate, you stop waiting for reasons to be grateful. You understand that gratitude itself creates the reason. You no longer postpone joy until conditions improve; you realize that joy is not a reaction but a way of seeing.

To celebrate is to live with open arms, not clinging to what has passed, not fearing what may come, but embracing this unfolding moment as part of a grand, unseen perfection. In that moment, life ceases to be a struggle and becomes a song. And you, no longer a mere participant, become the melody itself.

The Freedom Beyond Thoughts-

There comes a moment in every seeker's journey when the river of inquiry reaches the ocean of silence. After all the observation, all the surrender, all the celebration, what remains is not a new philosophy, but a simple, boundless stillness. This is the freedom beyond thoughts.

Freedom does not mean that the mind stops producing thoughts. The mind, like the heart, has its own rhythm; its nature is to move. Freedom means that your awareness no longer becomes entangled in that movement. You still think, but thinking no longer imprisons you. You still feel, but feelings no longer define you. You still act, but the actor, that restless center of "I", begins to dissolve.

When the clouds of thought no longer obscure the sky of awareness, what remains is luminous clarity, the sense of simply being. Being needs no reason, no justification, no conclusion. It is the original peace, untouched by gain or loss, untouched even by time. Thoughts may come and go, but awareness remains, unshaken, infinite, silently witnessing the play.

The mind, when unobserved, behaves like a storm, quick to form, eager to control, terrified of stillness. But when you begin to watch it with gentleness, its intensity softens. The very act of watching transforms the watcher. The current of thoughts continues to flow, yet now you float above it. You begin to understand that you were never the storm, you were the sky in which the storm appeared.

This recognition is liberation- the realization that nothing can truly bind you because nothing can touch what you are in essence. Fear loses its foundation here. It can knock on the door of your consciousness, but there is no one left to open. Pain can arise, but it cannot root. Thoughts can visit, but they cannot claim ownership. The mind becomes a garden where everything can bloom and fade naturally, without interference.

Freedom beyond thoughts is not a state of detachment or emptiness; it is fullness without grasping. It is the silence that holds every sound, the stillness that allows every movement. In this space, even the concept of "freedom" disappears, because there is no longer anyone to be bound.

You begin to see the world as it truly is, fluid, interconnected, alive. You see that joy and sorrow, gain and loss, birth and death are not opposites, but oscillations in one living field of consciousness. When awareness expands to include everything, exclusion ends, and with it ends the conflict that once defined human life.

This is the flowering of true intelligence- to live in the world fully, participate in it completely, yet remain inwardly untouched. You no longer chase permanence in the impermanent; you no longer run from uncertainty. You walk gently through the dream, knowing it for what it is, a play of divine energy through form.

And in that realization, the search itself ends. Not because you have found all the answers, but because you have outgrown the need for them. The one who was searching has merged back into the source. The drop has remembered it was never separate from the ocean.

Now, every breath feels sacred. Every moment feels sufficient. You can face the day with clarity, meet others with compassion, and rest at night with peace. Thoughts may rise and fall, but they no longer carry the weight of identity. You can smile at their coming and going, the way you smile at waves touching and leaving the shore.

This is not an escape from life, it is life itself, finally seen without distortion. It is the end of resistance, the birth of simplicity, the quiet arrival into what was always here.

The freedom beyond thoughts is not somewhere else. It is here, now, in the space between two breaths, in the pause before a word, in the stillness behind every sound. It waits for no achievement. It only waits for recognition.

And once recognized, it never leaves, because it was never absent.

AUTHOR'S PREFACE

When I first began to explore the landscape of fear, I did not imagine it would lead me here, to silence, to stillness, to love. Fear, for most of us, begins as a shadow we wish to escape. It seems to chase us through our ambitions, our relationships, and our restless nights. But over time, I discovered that fear is not an enemy to defeat; it is a doorway to enter. Behind that trembling door lies the greatest secret of life, that everything we resist is, in truth, trying to bring us home.

Through this journey, I realized that fear, pain, and uncertainty are not signs of weakness; they are signs that life is speaking to us in a language deeper than comfort. They remind us of our fragility, and through that reminder, they reveal our strength. They teach us to feel, to care, to grow.

When you stop running from fear and begin to listen to it, something miraculous happens. The same energy that once caused your heart to race becomes the rhythm of your awakening. The same thoughts that once haunted you begin to serve you, not as burdens, but as teachers. You start to see that life is not here to frighten you; it is here to expand you.

There were years when I tried to fight my own thoughts, to silence them, to replace them, to control them. It was only when I stopped fighting that I began to understand. The mind does not need to be silenced; it needs to be understood. Thoughts are not enemies; they are echoes of our evolution, reflections of our consciousness learning to see itself.

And when you see clearly, fear loses its authority. It becomes what it always was, movement within stillness, sound within silence, wave within ocean.

This book is not a manual to eliminate fear; it is an invitation to transform your relationship with it. Because fear, when understood, becomes awareness. Awareness, when deepened, becomes peace. And peace, when lived, becomes joy.

To live fearlessly is not to live without uncertainty, it is to live with trust. To surrender is not to give up, it is to give in to the wisdom that already knows. And to celebrate is not to deny life's storms, it is to dance through them, knowing the rain was never against you.

Every page of this book was born from my own journey, a journey of learning to breathe with life rather than against it. From the corridors of anxiety to the quiet light of meditation, from the noise of ambition to the simplicity of being, this path revealed that everything, even fear, was guiding me to the same truth- you are not your thoughts; you are the sky in which they move.

If there is one message I wish to leave with you, it is this- Life will never be fully predictable. The mind will never be fully silent. But your awareness, that witnessing presence behind every rise and fall, is already whole, already safe, already free.

So, the next time fear whispers in your ear, do not run.
Listen. Smile.
You are being reminded that you are alive, that your heart still cares, your mind still moves, your soul still learns.

Let fear come. Let it teach. Then let it go.
And when it does, celebrate.

Because in that moment, right there, between fear and freedom, you will meet the real essence of life.

ABOUT THE AUTHOR

Gajendra Singh Rathore is a thinker, meditator, and seeker who believes that the truest wisdom comes not from theories, but from direct experience. Over the past two decades, his journey has moved through many landscapes, from the structured world of technology and corporate success to the inward exploration of consciousness and the mysteries of the human mind.

What began as a personal battle with fear and overthinking gradually unfolded into a deeper understanding of life itself. Through years of meditation, observation, and introspection, he discovered that fear is not a flaw in human design, it is a force of evolution, a silent teacher guiding us toward awareness.

In his writings, Gajendra brings together psychology, philosophy, and lived experience to create reflections that are both profound and practical. His language is not that of a preacher or a philosopher, but of a fellow traveler, one who has walked through doubt, anxiety, and darkness and emerged with compassion, clarity, and a quiet joy.

He believes that true transformation begins when one stops running from their own thoughts and learns to sit with them, to listen, to understand, and finally, to celebrate them. Through his work, he hopes to help readers reconnect with their inner balance, rediscover their faith in life, and live with peace that no circumstance can disturb.

When not writing or meditating, Gajendra enjoys creating, exploring ideas, and connecting with people who seek meaning beyond the ordinary. His life's work is to remind others, and himself, that freedom is not found outside us, but within the stillness that has always been there.

www.ingramcontent.com/pod-product-compliance
Ingram Content Group UK Ltd.
Pitfield, Milton Keynes, MK11 3LW, UK
UKHW021343190726
13845UKWH00027B/700